Coding Step by Step

by Step

A Comprehensive
Handbook for Novice
Programmers

Jerry P. G. Bill

TABLE OF CONTENTS

Coding Step by Step

Coding Step by Step

Coding Step by Step

Coding Step by Step

Coding Step by Step

11

Coding Step by Step

Coding Step by Step

Introduction to Programming

What Is Programming?

Programming is the process of creating instructions that a computer can understand and execute to perform specific tasks. These instructions, known as "code," are written in programming languages, which serve as a medium of communication between humans and computers. Programming enables us to automate tasks, solve complex problems, build software, and power modern technologies.

At its core, programming is about problem-solving. A programmer identifies a problem, devises a logical solution, and translates that solution into code that computers can follow. Whether creating a simple calculator app or a sophisticated machine learning algorithm, programming involves breaking tasks into smaller, manageable steps and executing them efficiently.

Key benefits of programming include:

- Automating repetitive tasks.
- Building software applications and websites.
- Analyzing and processing vast amounts of data.
- Powering technological innovations like artificial intelligence and robotics.

Key Concepts and Terminologies

Before diving into programming, it's essential to understand some fundamental concepts and terminologies:

1. **Code**

   The set of instructions written in a programming language. It can range from simple commands to complex algorithms.

2. **Programming Languages**

   Tools used to write code. Examples include Python, JavaScript, Java, C++, and Ruby. Each language has its own syntax and use cases.

3. **Syntax**

   The set of rules defining how to write code in a particular programming language. Syntax errors occur when these rules are violated.

4. **Algorithm**

   A step-by-step procedure or formula for solving a problem.

5. **Compiler and Interpreter**

- A **compiler** translates the entire program into machine code before execution (e.g., C, C++).
- An **interpreter** translates code line-by-line during execution (e.g., Python, JavaScript).

6. **Variables**

   Containers used to store data. For example, $x = 5$ stores the value 5 in the variable x.

7. **Functions**

   Blocks of reusable code designed to perform a specific task. For example, a calculateSum() function might add two numbers.

8. **Loops**

   Constructs that repeat a block of code until a condition is met (e.g., for and while loops).

9. **Conditional Statements**

   Code that executes only if certain

conditions are true, such as if-else statements.

10. **Debugging**
The process of identifying and fixing errors or bugs in code.

11. **Integrated Development Environment (IDE)**
Software used for writing, editing, and debugging code, such as Visual Studio Code, PyCharm, or Eclipse.

12. **Source Code vs. Machine Code**

- **Source code** is human-readable and written by programmers.
- **Machine code** is binary (1s and 0s) and understood by computers.

Understanding these concepts lays the groundwork for writing and comprehending code effectively.

Choosing the Right Programming Language

With hundreds of programming languages available, choosing the right one depends on your goals, interests, and the type of projects you want to build. Here's a guide to help you decide:

1. **Beginner-Friendly Languages**

   - **Python**: Known for its simplicity and readability, ideal for beginners. Used in web development, data science, and AI.
   - **JavaScript**: Essential for web development. Allows you to create interactive websites.

2. **Languages for Software Development**

   - **Java**: Widely used for building enterprise applications, Android apps, and backend systems.
   - **C++**: Offers high performance, making it ideal for game development and systems programming.

3. Languages for Data Analysis and AI

- **R**: Preferred for statistical analysis and visualization.
- **Python**: Versatile and supports numerous libraries for AI and machine learning.

4. Languages for Web Development

- **HTML/CSS**: Not programming languages but essential for structuring and styling websites.
- **PHP**: Popular for server-side scripting.
- **JavaScript**: Used for both frontend and backend with frameworks like Node.js.

5. Languages for Mobile App Development

- **Swift**: Used for iOS development.
- **Kotlin**: The official language for Android development.

6. Languages for Embedded Systems

- ○ **C**: Lightweight and efficient, often used in embedded systems.

When choosing a language, consider factors like:

- The community and resources available (e.g., tutorials, forums).
- The type of projects you want to work on.
- Job opportunities in your chosen field.

Setting Up Your Development Environment

Before you start coding, setting up your development environment is crucial. A well-configured environment can significantly enhance productivity and reduce errors.

1. Choosing an IDE or Text Editor

- ○ **IDE**: Provides advanced tools like debugging, code autocompletion,

and project management (e.g., Visual Studio Code, IntelliJ IDEA).
- ○ **Text Editor**: Lightweight alternatives like Sublime Text or Notepad++ for simpler projects.

2. **Installing a Compiler or Interpreter**
Depending on the language, you might need additional tools:

- ○ For **Python**, download the interpreter from python.org.
- ○ For **Java**, install the JDK (Java Development Kit).
- ○ For **C++**, install compilers like GCC or Visual Studio.

3. **Version Control Tools**
Tools like **Git** allow you to track changes in your code and collaborate with others. Platforms like GitHub provide a space to host your repositories.

4. **Setting Up Dependencies**
Many programming languages use package managers to install libraries and

dependencies:

- ○ Python: pip
- ○ JavaScript: npm or yarn
- ○ Ruby: gem
5. **Configuring Your Environment**

- ○ Set up a proper directory structure for organizing your projects.
- ○ Configure your IDE or text editor with extensions or plugins for your language.
- ○ Enable syntax highlighting, linting, and debugging features.

Testing Your Setup
Write a "Hello, World!" program to ensure everything is working correctly. For example:

```
print("Hello, World!")
```

Once your development environment is ready, you're set to begin your programming journey with confidence.

Understanding Algorithms and Flowcharts

The Basics of Algorithms

An **algorithm** is a step-by-step set of instructions designed to perform a specific task or solve a particular problem. Algorithms are the backbone of programming, guiding the logical sequence of actions computers execute to achieve desired outcomes.

Key Characteristics of Algorithms

1. **Definiteness**: Every step in an algorithm must be clear and unambiguous.
2. **Finiteness**: An algorithm must have a finite number of steps, ensuring it terminates at some point.
3. **Input**: Algorithms accept zero or more inputs to process.
4. **Output**: They produce at least one output as a result.
5. **Effectiveness**: Each step must be feasible and accomplishable with available resources.

Example of an Algorithm: Adding Two Numbers

1. Start.
2. Input the first number (num1).
3. Input the second number (num2).
4. Calculate the sum of num1 and num2.
5. Output the result.
6. End.

Types of Algorithms

1. **Search Algorithms**: Find elements within a dataset (e.g., binary search).
2. **Sorting Algorithms**: Arrange data in a specific order (e.g., bubble sort, quicksort).
3. **Mathematical Algorithms**: Solve mathematical problems (e.g., Euclid's algorithm for GCD).
4. **Dynamic Programming Algorithms**: Break problems into smaller overlapping subproblems.
5. **Greedy Algorithms**: Make the most optimal choice at each step.

Why Algorithms Matter

- **Efficiency**: Good algorithms optimize resources like time and memory.
- **Reusability**: They can be applied to similar problems with minor adjustments.
- **Scalability**: Well-designed algorithms handle larger datasets effectively.

How to Create and Use Flowcharts

A **flowchart** is a graphical representation of an algorithm or process using symbols to depict steps and their relationships. Flowcharts make complex logic easier to understand and communicate, acting as a bridge between conceptual thinking and implementation.

Key Components of a Flowchart

1. **Symbols**:

   - **Oval (Terminator)**: Represents the start or end of a process.
   - **Rectangle (Process)**: Represents a step or action.
   - **Diamond (Decision)**: Represents a decision point with multiple outcomes.
   - **Arrow**: Shows the flow of control or sequence.
2. **Rules**:

- o Flowcharts should flow from top to bottom or left to right.
- o Each process symbol must connect to at least one other symbol.
- o Decision symbols must have two or more outgoing arrows for different outcomes.

Steps to Create a Flowchart

1. **Define the Purpose**: Identify the problem or process to visualize.
2. **List the Steps**: Write down each action or decision in the sequence they occur.
3. **Choose Symbols**: Use appropriate symbols for actions, decisions, and start/end points.
4. **Connect the Symbols**: Use arrows to show the logical flow.
5. **Review and Test**: Ensure the flowchart accurately represents the logic and is easy to follow.

Example Flowchart: Checking if a Number is Even or Odd

1. **Start**: Input a number.
2. **Decision**: Check if the number is divisible by 2.
    o If true, output "Even."
    o If false, output "Odd."
3. **End**.

Flowchart Representation:

[Start] --> [Input Number] --> [Is Number Divisible by 2?] --> Yes: [Output Even] --> [End]

--> No: [Output Odd] --> [End]

Applications of Flowcharts

- Designing software systems.
- Explaining algorithms to non-technical audiences.
- Documenting processes for business workflows.

Pseudocode: Bridging Ideas and Implementation

Pseudocode is an informal, plain-language description of the steps in an algorithm. It serves as an intermediate step between designing an algorithm and writing actual code. Pseudocode is not language-specific, making it a universal tool for programmers to convey logic without worrying about syntax.

Characteristics of Good Pseudocode

1. **Readable**: Easy for humans to understand, even those without programming knowledge.
2. **Structured**: Organized logically, often resembling the structure of code.
3. **Concise**: Focuses on the logic, omitting unnecessary details.
4. **Descriptive**: Clearly conveys the purpose of each step.

Writing Pseudocode

1. **Define Inputs and Outputs**: Clearly state what the algorithm receives and produces.
2. **Outline Key Steps**: Break the problem into small, manageable actions.
3. **Use Indentation**: Indent to show nested logic or hierarchical structure.
4. **Incorporate Control Structures**: Include loops (FOR, WHILE) and conditionals (IF, ELSE) as needed.

Example of Pseudocode: Finding the Largest of Three Numbers

BEGIN

  Input num1, num2, num3

  IF num1 > num2 AND num1 > num3 THEN

    Output "num1 is the largest"

  ELSE IF num2 > num1 AND num2 > num3
THEN

    Output "num2 is the largest"

  ELSE

Output "num3 is the largest"

ENDIF

END

Benefits of Pseudocode

- **Language Independence**: Allows focusing on logic rather than syntax.
- **Collaboration**: Facilitates communication between programmers and non-programmers.
- **Preparation**: Serves as a blueprint for actual coding.

Converting Pseudocode to Code

Once pseudocode is finalized, it can easily be translated into a programming language. For instance, the above example in Python would be:

```
num1 = int(input("Enter first number: "))
```

```
num2 = int(input("Enter second number: "))
```

```python
num3 = int(input("Enter third number: "))


if num1 > num2 and num1 > num3:

    print("num1 is the largest")
elif num2 > num1 and num2 > num3:

    print("num2 is the largest")
else:

    print("num3 is the largest")
```

Summary

- **Algorithms**: Provide a systematic approach to problem-solving. They must be clear, finite, and effective.
- **Flowcharts**: Visualize algorithms, making complex processes easier to understand and communicate.

- **Pseudocode**: Acts as a bridge between conceptual logic and actual implementation, promoting clarity and collaboration.

Mastering these tools equips you to design and implement solutions effectively, whether you're planning software systems or tackling coding challenges.

Programming Fundamentals

Programming fundamentals are the building blocks of any programming language. A firm grasp of these concepts is essential to understand and write efficient code.

Variables and Data Types

What Are Variables?

A **variable** is a named storage location in a computer's memory that holds a value. Variables act as containers for data that can be manipulated and reused during program execution.

For example:

age = 25

name = "Alice"

Here, age and name are variables storing an integer and a string, respectively.

Rules for Naming Variables

1. **Case-sensitive**: Variable names are case-sensitive (Name and name are different).
2. **Start with a Letter**: Names must begin with a letter or an underscore (_).
3. **No Special Characters**: Avoid spaces, symbols, or punctuation other than _ .

4. **Descriptive Names**: Use names that reflect the variable's purpose (temperature is better than t).

Data Types

Data types determine the kind of data a variable can hold. They vary slightly between programming languages but generally include:

1. **Numeric Types**:

   ○ **Integer (int)**: Whole numbers, e.g., 5, -100.
   ○ **Float**: Decimal numbers, e.g., 3.14, -0.01.

2. **Text Types**:

   ○ **String (str)**: A sequence of characters, e.g., "Hello World!".

3. **Boolean**:

   ○ **bool**: Represents truth values: True or False.

4. **Complex Types**:

   - **List/Array**: Ordered collections, e.g., [1, 2, 3].
   - **Dictionary/Map**: Key-value pairs, e.g., {"name": "Alice", "age": 25}.

5. **None/Null**:

   - Represents the absence of value, e.g., None in Python or null in JavaScript.

Declaring Variables in Popular Languages

Python:

x = 10

name = "Alice"

is_valid = True

- **Java**:

   int x = 10;

```
String name = "Alice";
```

```
boolean isValid = true;
```

- **JavaScript**:

```
let x = 10;
```

```
const name = "Alice";
```

```
var isValid = true;
```

Input and Output Operations

Input Operations

Input operations allow programs to receive data from users. This makes programs dynamic and interactive.

Input in Python:

```
name = input("Enter your name: ")
```

```
age = int(input("Enter your age: "))  # Converts
input to an integer
```

1.

Input in Java:

```
import java.util.Scanner;

Scanner scanner = new Scanner(System.in);

System.out.print("Enter your name: ");

String name = scanner.nextLine();

System.out.print("Enter your age: ");

int age = scanner.nextInt();
```

2.

Input in JavaScript (using HTML prompt):

```
let name = prompt("Enter your name:");

let age = parseInt(prompt("Enter your age:"));
```

3.

Output Operations

Output operations display data or messages to users.

Output in Python:

```
print("Hello, World!")
```

```
print(f"Your name is {name} and you are {age} years old.")
```

1.

Output in Java:

```
System.out.println("Hello, World!");
```

```
System.out.println("Your name is " + name + " and you are " + age + " years old.");
```

2.

Output in JavaScript:

```
console.log("Hello, World!");

alert(`Your name is ${name} and you are ${age}
years old.`);
```

Operators and Expressions

What Are Operators?

Operators are symbols or keywords used to perform operations on variables and values. They are the building blocks for creating expressions.

Types of Operators

1. **Arithmetic Operators**: Perform basic mathematical operations.

- Addition (+), Subtraction (-), Multiplication (*), Division (/), Modulus (%).

Example:
 result = 10 + 5 # Output: 15

remainder = 10 % 3 # Output: 1

2. **Comparison (Relational) Operators**: Compare two values, returning a Boolean (True or False).

- Equal to (==), Not equal to (!=), Greater than (>), Less than (<), Greater than or equal to (>=), Less than or equal to (<=).

Example:
 is_equal = (5 == 5) # Output: True

is_greater = (10 > 5) # Output: True

3. **Logical Operators**: Combine multiple
   conditions.

   ○ AND (and or &&), OR (or or ||),
     NOT (not or !).

Example:
 condition = (5 > 3 and 10 > 5) # Output: True

4. **Assignment Operators**: Assign values to
   variables.

   ○ Simple (=), Add and assign (+=),
     Subtract and assign (-=), etc.

Example:
 x = 10

x += 5 # Equivalent to x = x + 5

5. **Bitwise Operators**: Perform operations at the bit level.

   ○ AND (&), OR (|), XOR (^), Left Shift (<<), Right Shift (>>).
6. **Membership Operators** (specific to some languages like Python):

   ○ in and not in check for membership in a sequence.

Example:
 fruits = ["apple", "banana"]

is_present = "apple" in fruits # Output: True

What Are Expressions?

An **expression** is a combination of variables, values, and operators that evaluates to a value.
 Example:

x = 5

y = 10

z = x + y # Expression: x + y

Order of Precedence

The order in which operators are evaluated in expressions is critical. Most languages follow this precedence:

1. Parentheses (()).
2. Exponents (** in Python).
3. Multiplication, Division, Modulus.
4. Addition, Subtraction.
5. Comparison.
6. Logical.

Control Structures

Control structures are fundamental programming constructs that allow programmers to control the flow of execution within a program. They enable decision-making, repetition, and organization of logic, transforming simple instructions into powerful algorithms that solve complex problems.

Decision-Making: If, Else, and Switch

The If Statement

The if statement allows a program to make decisions based on a condition. If the condition evaluates to True, the code block inside the if statement is executed. Otherwise, it is skipped.

Syntax (Python):

if condition:

    # Code to execute if the condition is True

Example (Python):

age = 20

if age >= 18:

    print("You are an adult.")

Here, the program checks if age is greater than or equal to 18. Since age is 20, the message "You are an adult." is printed.

The Else Statement

The else statement works in conjunction with the if statement. It defines an alternative code block that runs when the condition is False.

Syntax (Python):

```
if condition:

    # Code to execute if the condition is True

else:

    # Code to execute if the condition is False
```

Example (Python):

```
age = 16

if age >= 18:

    print("You are an adult.")

else:

    print("You are a minor.")
```

Since age is 16, the program prints "You are a minor."

The Elif Statement (Else If)

The elif (else if) statement allows for multiple conditions to be checked sequentially. It is useful when there are more than two possible outcomes.

Syntax (Python):

if condition1:

   # Code for condition1

elif condition2:

   # Code for condition2

else:

   # Code if all conditions fail

Example (Python):

```
age = 70

if age < 18:

    print("You are a minor.")

elif age >= 18 and age <= 65:

    print("You are an adult.")

else:

    print("You are a senior citizen.")
```

This program checks multiple age ranges and prints the appropriate message.

The Switch Statement (or Case in some languages)

The switch statement (used in languages like C, Java, JavaScript) is an alternative to multiple if-elif statements. It is used when you need to compare the same variable or expression against multiple possible values.

Syntax (C/C++/Java/JavaScript):

```
switch (expression) {

    case value1:

        // Code for value1

        break;

    case value2:

        // Code for value2

        break;

    default:

        // Code for default case

}
```

Example (JavaScript):

```
let day = 3;

switch (day) {
```

```
case 1:

    console.log("Monday");

    break;

case 2:

    console.log("Tuesday");

    break;

case 3:

    console.log("Wednesday");

    break;

default:

    console.log("Invalid day");

}
```

In this case, since day equals 3, the program prints "Wednesday."

Loops: For, While, and Do-While

The For Loop

The for loop is used when you know the number of times you need to iterate through a block of code. It is typically used for iterating over a range of values or items in a collection like an array or list.

Syntax (Python):

for i in range(start, end, step):

    # Code to execute in each iteration

Example (Python):

for i in range(1, 6):

    print(i)

This prints numbers 1 through 5, as range(1, 6) generates numbers from 1 to 5.

The While Loop

The while loop executes a block of code repeatedly as long as a condition is True. It is typically used when the number of iterations is not known in advance and the loop continues until a condition is met.

Syntax (Python):

while condition:

    # Code to execute as long as the condition is True

Example (Python):

count = 1

while count <= 5:

    print(count)

count += 1

This loop will print numbers from 1 to 5. The condition count <= 5 is checked before each iteration, and the loop continues as long as the condition is True.

The Do-While Loop

The do-while loop, found in languages like C, C++, and Java, executes a block of code at least once and then checks the condition after the first iteration. This guarantees that the loop body is executed at least once, even if the condition is False initially.

Syntax (C/C++/Java):

do {

   // Code to execute

} while (condition);

Example (Java):

```
int count = 1;

do {

    System.out.println(count);

    count++;

} while (count <= 5);
```

This will also print numbers from 1 to 5, but the key difference is that the loop body is executed at least once, regardless of the condition.

Nested and Complex Control Structures

Nested If Statements

You can nest if statements inside other if statements to check multiple conditions. This allows more complex decision-making logic.

Example (Python):

```python
age = 20
if age >= 18:
    if age <= 30:
        print("You are a young adult.")
    else:
        print("You are an adult.")
```

Here, the program checks two conditions: whether age is greater than or equal to 18, and whether it is less than or equal to 30.

Nested Loops

Nested loops are loops inside other loops. They are commonly used when working with multi-dimensional data structures, such as matrices or arrays of arrays.

Example (Python):

```
for i in range(1, 4):

    for j in range(1, 4):

        print(f"i = {i}, j = {j}")
```

This prints:

i = 1, j = 1

i = 1, j = 2

i = 1, j = 3

i = 2, j = 1

i = 2, j = 2

i = 2, j = 3

i = 3, j = 1

i = 3, j = 2

i = 3, j = 3

In this example, the outer loop iterates over i, while the inner loop iterates over j for each value of i.

Complex Control Structures

Complex control structures involve combining multiple decision-making and loop constructs in one program. These structures allow you to solve intricate problems by evaluating multiple conditions and iterating through data structures.

Example (Python):

```python
number = 5

if number > 0:

    for i in range(1, number + 1):

        if i % 2 == 0:

            print(f"{i} is even")

        else:

            print(f"{i} is odd")
```

Here, the program first checks if number is positive. Then, it loops from 1 to number and prints whether each number is even or odd.

Summary

Control structures are integral to programming, enabling dynamic decision-making and repetition of code. Mastering the if, else, switch, and looping constructs (for, while, and do-while) is crucial for writing efficient, organized, and readable code. Combining simple control structures into nested and complex forms allows programmers to solve more advanced problems and create powerful algorithms.

Functions and Modular Programming

In programming, functions serve as essential building blocks that allow you to organize, reuse, and modularize your code. A function is a self-contained block of code designed to accomplish a specific task. Functions can be defined once and called multiple times, which helps reduce redundancy and improve the readability and maintainability of a program. In this section, we will explore how to define and call functions, the role of function parameters and return values, and the concept of recursion—functions that call themselves.

Defining and Calling Functions

What is a Function?

A function is a named block of code that performs a specific task. Functions help organize programs into smaller, manageable pieces. By grouping code into functions, you can enhance readability, reduce redundancy, and make your program more modular and maintainable.

Defining a Function

To define a function, you typically use a keyword like def in Python or function in JavaScript. The function definition includes a name, an optional list of parameters, and the body of the function that contains the instructions to be executed.

Syntax (Python):

def function_name():

```
# Code block

print("Hello, World!")
```

Example (Python):

```
def greet():

    print("Hello, World!")
```

In this example, we defined a function greet() that prints "Hello, World!" when called.

Calling a Function

To use the function you've defined, you call it by its name followed by parentheses ().

Example (Python):

```
greet()  # This will call the function and print "Hello, World!"
```

When greet() is called, the program jumps to the function definition and executes the code within the body, printing "Hello, World!" in this case.

Returning from a Function

A function can also return a value using the return keyword. The value returned by the function can be stored in a variable or used directly in expressions.

Syntax (Python):

```
def add(a, b):

    return a + b
```

Example (Python):

```
result = add(3, 5)

print(result)  # This will print 8
```

Here, the function add takes two parameters (a and b) and returns their sum. The returned value is then stored in the variable result.

Function Parameters and Return Values

Function Parameters

Parameters are values passed into a function when it is called. These values are used inside the function body to perform the desired task. Parameters make functions flexible, allowing them to work with different inputs.

Syntax (Python):

```
def function_name(parameter1, parameter2):

    # Code using the parameters
```

Example (Python):

```
def greet(name):
```

```
print(f"Hello, {name}!")
```

```
greet("Alice")  # This will print "Hello, Alice!"
```

In this case, name is a parameter. When calling greet("Alice"), the string "Alice" is passed into the function, and the program prints "Hello, Alice!".

Default Parameters

In some cases, you may want to provide a default value for a parameter. If the caller doesn't pass a value, the function will use the default.

Example (Python):

```
def greet(name="Guest"):

   print(f"Hello, {name}!")
```

```
greet("Bob")  # This will print "Hello, Bob!"
```

greet()   # This will print "Hello, Guest!"

Here, if no argument is passed to greet(), the default value "Guest" is used.

Return Values

A function can return a result using the return keyword. Once a function returns a value, the function execution stops, and the value is sent back to the caller. A function can return any type of value, such as a number, string, list, or even another function.

Example (Python):

```
def multiply(x, y):

    return x * y


result = multiply(4, 5)

print(result)  # This will print 20
```

In this example, the function multiply takes two arguments x and y, multiplies them, and returns the result. The returned value is assigned to the variable result, which is then printed.

Recursion: Functions That Call Themselves

What is Recursion?

Recursion is a programming concept where a function calls itself in order to solve a problem. Recursion allows problems to be broken down into smaller, more manageable subproblems. While recursion is a powerful tool, it is important to ensure that there is a base case (a stopping condition) to prevent infinite recursion.

Basic Structure of a Recursive Function

A recursive function typically has two key parts:

1. **Base case**: The condition under which the function stops calling itself and returns a value.
2. **Recursive case**: The part where the function calls itself with a modified argument to move closer to the base case.

Syntax (Python):

```python
def recursive_function(parameters):

    if base_condition:  # Base case: stop condition

        return base_value

    else:

        # Recursive case: function calls itself

        return recursive_function(modified_parameters)
```

Example: Factorial Function

The factorial of a number n is the product of all positive integers less than or equal to n. The

factorial of 0 is defined as 1 (0! = 1). The
recursive formula for the factorial is:

- factorial(n) = n * factorial(n-1) for n > 0
- factorial(0) = 1

Example (Python):

```
def factorial(n):

    if n == 0:  # Base case

        return 1

    else:

        return n * factorial(n - 1)  # Recursive call


result = factorial(5)

print(result)  # This will print 120 (5! = 5 * 4 * 3
* 2 * 1)
```

In this example, the function factorial calls itself with decreasing values of n until n reaches 0, at which point the base case is met, and the function returns 1. The recursive calls then combine the results to produce the final answer.

Example: Fibonacci Sequence

Another classic example of recursion is the calculation of Fibonacci numbers. The Fibonacci sequence is defined as:

- $F(0) = 0$
- $F(1) = 1$
- $F(n) = F(n-1) + F(n-2)$ for $n > 1$

Example (Python):

```python
def fibonacci(n):

    if n == 0:

        return 0

    elif n == 1:

        return 1
```

```
    else:

        return fibonacci(n - 1) + fibonacci(n - 2)


result = fibonacci(6)

print(result)  # This will print 8 (Fibonacci
sequence: 0, 1, 1, 2, 3, 5, 8)
```

This example calculates the Fibonacci number for $n = 6$ by recursively summing the two preceding Fibonacci numbers.

When to Use Recursion

Recursion is particularly useful for problems that can naturally be divided into smaller subproblems, such as:

- Tree and graph traversal
- Divide-and-conquer algorithms (e.g., quicksort, mergesort)
- Factorial and Fibonacci calculations

- Solving puzzles like the Tower of Hanoi

However, recursion should be used cautiously as it can lead to performance issues if the recursion depth is too large or if the base case is not reached quickly.

Modular Programming

What is Modular Programming?

Modular programming refers to breaking down a program into smaller, independent modules (functions or classes) that can be developed, tested, and debugged separately. Each module handles a specific part of the task, and these modules work together to solve the overall problem.

Advantages of Modular Programming:

- **Reusability**: Functions can be reused across different parts of the program or even in other programs.

- **Maintainability**: Bugs are easier to find and fix in small modules.
- **Readability**: Programs are easier to understand when broken into logical, smaller pieces.

Example (Python):

```
# Module 1: Function to add two numbers

def add(x, y):

    return x + y



# Module 2: Function to subtract two numbers

def subtract(x, y):

    return x - y



# Main Program

def main():
```

```
result1 = add(10, 5)

result2 = subtract(10, 5)

print(f"Sum: {result1}, Difference:
{result2}")


main()
```

In this example, the program is divided into two modules (add and subtract functions). The main() function brings them together and uses them.

Summary

Functions are one of the most important concepts in programming, allowing you to break your code into manageable, reusable, and testable blocks. Understanding how to define, call, and use functions—along with handling parameters, return values, and recursion—enables you to write clean, efficient, and maintainable code. Modular programming complements this by promoting the organization of code into smaller units that can be developed and maintained independently, leading to improved productivity and code quality.

Object-Oriented Programming (OOP)

Object-Oriented Programming (OOP) is a programming paradigm that revolves around the concept of objects, which are instances of classes. In OOP, the focus shifts from writing procedures (functions) to organizing and modeling data and behavior into reusable structures called "objects." OOP provides a framework for developers to create modular, maintainable, and scalable software. It is widely used in software development today, particularly in large-scale applications and systems.

In this section, we will explore the fundamental principles of OOP: classes and objects, inheritance and polymorphism, encapsulation and abstraction.

Introduction to OOP Concepts

Object-Oriented Programming is built upon four key principles: **Encapsulation, Abstraction, Inheritance**, and **Polymorphism**. These principles help organize code in a way that makes it easier to manage and maintain, especially as projects grow in complexity.

1. **Encapsulation**: The idea of bundling data (variables) and methods (functions) into a single unit called a class. It also involves restricting direct access to some of the object's components and only allowing modification through well-defined methods (getters and setters).

2. **Abstraction**: Abstraction involves hiding the complex reality of the system and exposing only the necessary parts. In

OOP, it allows a programmer to interact with an object without needing to understand all the internal workings of that object.

3. **Inheritance**: Inheritance allows one class to inherit the attributes and behaviors (methods) of another class. This encourages code reuse and can represent "is-a" relationships between objects.

4. **Polymorphism**: Polymorphism means "many forms." It allows objects of different classes to be treated as objects of a common superclass. Through polymorphism, methods can be used in the same way across different types of objects, simplifying the interface and allowing for more flexible code.

Classes and Objects

What is a Class?

A class is a blueprint or template for creating objects. It defines the properties (attributes) and behaviors (methods or functions) that an object will have. A class can be thought of as a mold from which objects (instances) are created.

Syntax (Python):

```python
class Car:

    # Attributes (properties)

    def __init__(self, brand, model, year):

        self.brand = brand

        self.model = model

        self.year = year


    # Method (behavior)

    def drive(self):
```

```
    print(f"The {self.brand} {self.model} is
driving.")
```

Here, Car is a class that defines the properties of
a car (brand, model, year) and its behavior
(drive() method).

What is an Object?

An object is an instance of a class. When a class
is defined, no memory is allocated. However,
when an object is created, memory is allocated,
and it holds the actual data. Each object can have
its own values for the class's attributes.

Syntax (Python):

```
# Creating an object (instance) of the Car class

my_car = Car("Toyota", "Corolla", 2020)

my_car.drive()  # Output: The Toyota Corolla is
driving.
```

In this example, my_car is an object of the Car class. It has its own values for brand, model, and year, and it can use the drive() method defined in the class.

Constructor (__init__)

In Python, the __init__ method is a special method known as the constructor. It is automatically called when an object is instantiated. It is used to initialize the object's attributes.

Example:

```
class Book:

    def __init__(self, title, author, pages):

        self.title = title

        self.author = author

        self.pages = pages
```

```
my_book = Book("The Great Gatsby", "F. Scott
Fitzgerald", 180)

print(my_book.title)  # Output: The Great
Gatsby
```

Inheritance and Polymorphism

What is Inheritance?

Inheritance is the mechanism by which a class can inherit the attributes and methods of another class. The class that inherits from another class is called a **child class** or **subclass**, while the class being inherited from is called the **parent class** or **superclass**. Inheritance promotes code reuse and establishes a hierarchy between classes.

Example (Python):

```
# Parent class (Superclass)
```

```python
class Animal:

    def __init__(self, name):

        self.name = name


    def speak(self):

        pass  # A placeholder method to be overridden by subclasses


# Child class (Subclass)

class Dog(Animal):

    def speak(self):

        print(f"{self.name} says Woof!")


# Child class (Subclass)

class Cat(Animal):
```

```
def speak(self):

    print(f"{self.name} says Meow!")
```

```
# Creating objects of the subclasses

dog = Dog("Rex")

cat = Cat("Whiskers")
```

```
dog.speak()  # Output: Rex says Woof!

cat.speak()  # Output: Whiskers says Meow!
```

In this example, Dog and Cat inherit from the Animal class. The speak() method is overridden in both subclasses to provide specific behavior for each animal.

Polymorphism

Polymorphism allows different classes to have methods with the same name but with different implementations. It enables objects of different classes to be treated as objects of a common superclass. The main benefit of polymorphism is that it provides a unified interface for working with different objects.

There are two types of polymorphism:

1. **Method Overriding**: A subclass provides its own implementation of a method defined in the parent class.
2. **Method Overloading**: A method is defined multiple times with different numbers or types of parameters.

Example (Python) - Method Overriding:

```
class Shape:

    def area(self):

        pass  # A placeholder method
```

```python
class Circle(Shape):

    def __init__(self, radius):

        self.radius = radius


    def area(self):

        return 3.14 * (self.radius ** 2)


class Rectangle(Shape):

    def __init__(self, width, height):

        self.width = width

        self.height = height


    def area(self):

        return self.width * self.height
```

Using Polymorphism

shapes = [Circle(5), Rectangle(3, 4)]

for shape in shapes:

   print(f"Area: {shape.area()}")

In this example, both Circle and Rectangle classes implement the area() method, but with different formulas. The area() method is polymorphic, as it behaves differently depending on the object type (Circle or Rectangle).

Encapsulation and Abstraction

What is Encapsulation?

Encapsulation refers to the bundling of data (attributes) and methods (functions) that operate on the data within a single unit, i.e., a class. It is the practice of restricting direct access to some of the object's attributes or methods. This is done by marking certain attributes or methods as **private** and exposing public methods (getters and setters) to interact with the object's internal state.

Example (Python):

```python
class BankAccount:

    def __init__(self, balance=0):

        self.__balance = balance  # Private attribute


    def deposit(self, amount):

        if amount > 0:

            self.__balance += amount

        else:

            print("Deposit amount must be positive.")
```

```
def get_balance(self):

    return self.__balance
```

```
# Create a BankAccount object

account = BankAccount(100)

account.deposit(50)

print(account.get_balance())  # Output: 150
```

In this example, the __balance attribute is encapsulated within the BankAccount class. It is made private by convention, and we interact with it only through public methods (deposit() and get_balance()).

What is Abstraction?

Abstraction is the concept of hiding the complex implementation details and showing only the essential features of an object. It is closely related to encapsulation but focuses more on simplifying the interface by providing a high-level view of the object's capabilities, rather than the intricate details of its implementation.

Example (Python):

```python
from abc import ABC, abstractmethod


class Shape(ABC):

    @abstractmethod
    def area(self):
        pass


class Square(Shape):
    def __init__(self, side):
        self.side = side
```

```python
    def area(self):

        return self.side ** 2


class Circle(Shape):

    def __init__(self, radius):

        self.radius = radius


    def area(self):

        return 3.14 * self.radius ** 2


# Using abstraction

shapes = [Square(4), Circle(5)]

for shape in shapes:

    print(f"Area: {shape.area()}")
```

Here, the Shape class is abstract, meaning it cannot be instantiated. The area() method is abstract, forcing subclasses (Square and Circle) to implement their specific behavior. The user only interacts with the high-level area() method, abstracting away the specific details.

Summary

Object-Oriented Programming is a powerful programming paradigm that promotes the organization of code into logical structures that mimic real-world entities and their interactions. The core concepts of OOP—classes and objects, inheritance, polymorphism, encapsulation, and abstraction—empower developers to write modular, reusable, and maintainable code. By understanding and applying these OOP principles, programmers can build more efficient and scalable applications.

Working with Data Structures

Data structures are fundamental tools used to organize and store data in a way that allows for efficient access and manipulation. The choice of data structure can significantly impact the performance of a program, especially as the amount of data grows. In this section, we will explore several essential data structures: **Arrays and Lists, Stacks and Queues, Linked Lists,** and **Hash Tables and Dictionaries**. Each of these data structures has unique characteristics and is suited to particular types of operations.

Arrays and Lists

What are Arrays?

An array is a collection of elements, typically of the same data type, stored in contiguous memory locations. Each element in the array can be accessed by its index, making arrays a fast and efficient data structure for indexing and retrieving data. Arrays are often used when the number of elements is known in advance, and the elements need to be accessed randomly.

Key Properties:

- Fixed size: Once the array is created, its size cannot be changed.
- Index-based access: Elements can be accessed using an index (usually starting from 0).
- Efficient for accessing elements by index but can be inefficient for inserting or deleting elements in the middle.

Syntax (Python):

```
# Defining an array (in Python, a list is used to
represent an array)

my_array = [1, 2, 3, 4, 5]


# Accessing elements by index

print(my_array[0])  # Output: 1
```

What are Lists?

A list in many programming languages (like Python) is a dynamic array that can grow or shrink in size. Unlike an array, a list can store elements of different data types. Lists are more flexible than arrays but may have performance trade-offs, especially when it comes to large datasets.

Key Properties:

- Dynamic size: Lists can grow or shrink in size as elements are added or removed.

- Can store heterogeneous data types.
- Slower than arrays for indexing but more flexible for adding/removing elements.

Syntax (Python):

```
my_list = [1, "hello", 3.14, True]
```

```
# Accessing elements

print(my_list[1])  # Output: "hello"
```

Differences Between Arrays and Lists:

- **Arrays** are fixed in size and optimized for indexing, whereas **lists** are dynamic and can store elements of different data types.
- **Lists** in languages like Python are more flexible, while **arrays** are typically faster for tasks like element retrieval, especially in statically typed languages like C and Java.

Stacks and Queues

What is a Stack?

A **stack** is a linear data structure that follows the **Last In, First Out (LIFO)** principle. This means the most recently added element is the first one to be removed. Stacks are commonly used for tasks like undo functionality in applications, parsing expressions, or managing function calls in programming.

Key Operations:

- **Push**: Add an element to the top of the stack.
- **Pop**: Remove the top element from the stack.
- **Peek**: Retrieve the top element without removing it.
- **IsEmpty**: Check if the stack is empty.

Syntax (Python):

Creating a stack using a list

```
stack = []


# Push elements

stack.append(1)

stack.append(2)

stack.append(3)


# Pop elements

print(stack.pop())  # Output: 3


# Peek at the top element

print(stack[-1])  # Output: 2
```

What is a Queue?

A **queue** is a linear data structure that follows the **First In, First Out (FIFO)** principle. This means the first element added to the queue is the first one to be removed. Queues are often used for tasks such as scheduling processes in operating systems or handling requests in web servers.

Key Operations:

- **Enqueue**: Add an element to the rear of the queue.
- **Dequeue**: Remove an element from the front of the queue.
- **Peek**: Retrieve the front element without removing it.
- **IsEmpty**: Check if the queue is empty.

Syntax (Python):

from collections import deque

Creating a queue using deque

```python
queue = deque()

# Enqueue elements

queue.append(1)

queue.append(2)

queue.append(3)


# Dequeue elements

print(queue.popleft())  # Output: 1


# Peek at the front element

print(queue[0])  # Output: 2
```

Differences Between Stacks and Queues:

- **Stack** follows the LIFO principle, whereas a **queue** follows the FIFO principle.
- In a **stack**, the last element pushed is the first one to be popped, while in a **queue**, the first element enqueued is the first one to be dequeued.

Linked Lists

What is a Linked List?

A **linked list** is a linear data structure in which elements (called nodes) are not stored in contiguous memory locations. Each node contains two parts: data and a reference (or link) to the next node in the sequence. Linked lists are dynamic, meaning they can grow or shrink in size during runtime.

Types of Linked Lists:

1. **Singly Linked List**: Each node contains data and a reference to the next node.

2. **Doubly Linked List**: Each node contains data and references to both the next and the previous nodes.
3. **Circular Linked List**: The last node points back to the first node, forming a circular structure.

Key Operations:

- **Insert**: Add a new node to the list.
- **Delete**: Remove a node from the list.
- **Traverse**: Visit each node in the list.

Syntax (Python):

```python
# Node class

class Node:

    def __init__(self, data):

        self.data = data

        self.next = None


# LinkedList class
```

```python
class LinkedList:

    def __init__(self):

        self.head = None


    def append(self, data):

        new_node = Node(data)

        if not self.head:

            self.head = new_node

        else:

            current = self.head

            while current.next:

                current = current.next

            current.next = new_node


    def display(self):
```

```python
        current = self.head

        while current:

            print(current.data, end=" -> ")

            current = current.next

        print()


# Create and display a linked list

linked_list = LinkedList()

linked_list.append(1)

linked_list.append(2)

linked_list.append(3)

linked_list.display()  # Output: 1 -> 2 -> 3 ->
```

Advantages of Linked Lists:

- Dynamic size: Linked lists can grow or shrink in size as needed.
- Efficient insertions/deletions: Inserting or deleting elements (especially at the beginning or middle) is faster than in arrays.

Disadvantages of Linked Lists:

- Sequential access: To access an element at a specific position, you must traverse the list from the beginning.
- Extra memory usage: Each node requires additional memory for the reference to the next node.

Hash Tables and Dictionaries

What is a Hash Table?

A **hash table** is a data structure that stores key-value pairs and uses a hash function to compute an index (or hash) into an array of buckets or slots, from which the desired value can be found. Hash tables are used to implement associative arrays, sets, and databases, allowing for fast access to values when the key is known.

Key Operations:

- **Insert**: Add a key-value pair to the table.
- **Delete**: Remove a key-value pair from the table.
- **Search**: Find a value associated with a given key.

Hash Function: A function that takes an input (or "key") and returns an integer that is used to index into the table.

Syntax (Python - Dictionary):

Creating a hash table using a dictionary

my_dict = {"apple": 1, "banana": 2, "cherry": 3}

Accessing values by key

print(my_dict["banana"]) # Output: 2

```
# Adding new key-value pairs

my_dict["date"] = 4


# Removing key-value pairs

del my_dict["apple"]


# Checking for a key

print("banana" in my_dict)  # Output: True
```

Advantages of Hash Tables:

- **Fast access**: Hash tables provide constant-time average case complexity for search, insert, and delete operations.
- **Flexible**: They can store a wide range of data types as values.

Disadvantages of Hash Tables:

- **Collisions**: Two keys may hash to the same index, causing a collision. Handling collisions efficiently (e.g., chaining or open addressing) is crucial.
- **Inefficient for small data**: Hash tables may not be efficient for small datasets due to the overhead of the hash function and table resizing.

What are Dictionaries?

In Python, dictionaries are implemented as hash tables. They provide a simple and efficient way to store key-value pairs and offer all the functionalities of a hash table.

File Handling

File handling is an essential part of many programs, as it allows for storing, retrieving, and manipulating data outside of the memory of a program. It provides a way to save user inputs, configurations, logs, and much more, making programs persistent. In this section, we will cover the basics of **Reading and Writing Files**, **File Formats and Serialization**, and **Error Handling in File Operations**. Mastering file handling is a crucial skill for any programmer working with data that needs to be stored or transferred between systems.

Reading and Writing Files

File operations are the backbone of most programs that interact with the outside world. These operations enable us to open, read, write, and close files, either text or binary, in an efficient manner. The two most basic file operations are **reading** from and **writing** to files.

Opening Files

Before you can read from or write to a file, you need to open it. When a file is opened, the operating system provides a file handler (or file descriptor) which is used to interact with the file. In most programming languages, files can be opened in different modes based on what action you want to perform.

Common Modes:

- **r**: Read-only mode. Opens the file for reading.
- **w**: Write mode. Opens the file for writing (creates a new file or truncates an existing file).

- **a**: Append mode. Opens the file for appending data to the end.
- **rb**: Read mode for binary files.
- **wb**: Write mode for binary files.
- **r+**: Read and write mode.

Syntax (Python):

Opening a file in read mode

file = open("example.txt", "r")

Opening a file in write mode

file = open("example.txt", "w")

Reading Files

Reading files involves fetching the data stored in the file. There are various methods to read a file's content.

1. **read()**: Reads the entire file content into a single string.

2. **readline()**: Reads one line from the file at a time.
3. **readlines()**: Reads all lines from the file and returns them as a list of strings.

Syntax (Python):

Read entire content

with open("example.txt", "r") as file:

   content = file.read()

   print(content)

Read line by line

with open("example.txt", "r") as file:

   line = file.readline()

   while line:

     print(line.strip()) # strip() removes leading/trailing whitespaces line = file.readline()

Writing to Files

Writing data to a file involves opening the file in the appropriate mode (usually "w" or "a") and then using write operations to store data.

- **write()**: Writes a string to the file.
- **writelines()**: Writes a list of strings to the file.

Syntax (Python):

Writing data to a file

with open("output.txt", "w") as file:

file.write("Hello, world!")

Writing multiple lines

lines = ["Hello, world!\n", "Welcome to file handling!\n"]

```
with open("output.txt", "w") as file:

    file.writelines(lines)
```

Closing Files

After performing operations on a file, it's important to close the file to free system resources and ensure that changes are committed to the file.

Syntax (Python):

```
file = open("example.txt", "r")

# Perform file operations

file.close()
```

Using with Statement: In Python, it's recommended to use the with statement when working with files. This ensures that the file is automatically closed, even if an error occurs during file operations.

```
with open("example.txt", "r") as file:

    content = file.read()

    print(content)
```

File Formats and Serialization

What is Serialization?

Serialization is the process of converting an object or data structure into a format that can be easily stored in a file or transmitted over a network. Deserialization is the reverse process, where the serialized data is converted back into an object or data structure.

Serialization is particularly useful when you need to store more complex data structures (such as objects, lists, or dictionaries) to disk and later retrieve them without losing the data's integrity.

Common File Formats

- **Text Files (.txt)**: Simple text format, where data is written in plain text. It is human-readable but not ideal for complex data.
- **CSV Files (.csv)**: Comma-separated values are used to store tabular data in plain text. It's widely used in data analysis, and each line typically represents a row in the table.
- **JSON Files (.json)**: JavaScript Object Notation is a lightweight data-interchange format that is easy for humans to read and write and easy for machines to parse and generate. It's ideal for transmitting data between systems.
- **XML Files (.xml)**: Extensible Markup Language is a widely used format for structured data that can be both human-readable and machine-readable.

Serialization in Python (Pickle)

Python's pickle module is used for serializing and deserializing objects. It allows Python objects to be converted to a byte stream and then written to a file.

Syntax (Python - Pickle):

```
import pickle


# Serialization (Pickling)

data = {"name": "Alice", "age": 25}

with open("data.pkl", "wb") as file:

    pickle.dump(data, file)


# Deserialization (Unpickling)

with open("data.pkl", "rb") as file:

    loaded_data = pickle.load(file)
```

```
    print(loaded_data)  # Output: {'name': 'Alice',
'age': 25}
```

Serialization with JSON

JSON is a widely supported and portable format, making it ideal for exchanging data between different systems or storing data in a human-readable format.

Syntax (Python - JSON):

```
import json
```

```
# Serialization (JSON)

data = {"name": "Alice", "age": 25}

with open("data.json", "w") as file:

    json.dump(data, file)
```

```
# Deserialization (JSON)

with open("data.json", "r") as file:

    loaded_data = json.load(file)

    print(loaded_data)  # Output: {'name': 'Alice',
'age': 25}
```

Error Handling in File Operations

File handling often involves dealing with external systems, which may fail for various reasons, such as missing files, permission issues, or file corruption. Error handling ensures that your program can respond to such failures gracefully.

Common File-Related Errors

1. **FileNotFoundError**: Raised when attempting to open a file that does not exist.

2. **PermissionError**: Raised when trying to read/write a file without proper permissions.
3. **IsADirectoryError**: Raised when trying to open a directory as a file.
4. **IOError**: A general input/output error that can occur during file operations.

Using Try and Except Blocks

In Python, file handling errors can be managed using try, except, else, and finally blocks.

Example (Python):

```python
try:

    with open("example.txt", "r") as file:

        content = file.read()

        print(content)

except FileNotFoundError:

    print("Error: The file does not exist.")

except PermissionError:
```

```
    print("Error: Permission denied.")

except Exception as e:

    print(f"An unexpected error occurred: {e}")

finally:

    print("File operation completed.")
```

Handling Specific Errors

It's a good practice to catch specific exceptions first, followed by a generic Exception to capture any unexpected errors.

- **FileNotFoundError**: Raised if the specified file does not exist.
- **PermissionError**: Raised if the program does not have permission to access the file.
- **IOError**: General errors related to I/O operations, like a hardware failure.

Ensuring Safe File Access (Context Manager)

Using the with statement as a context manager automatically handles the opening and closing of files, ensuring resources are freed even if an error occurs.

```
try:

    with open("example.txt", "r") as file:

        content = file.read()

except FileNotFoundError:

    print("The file was not found.")
```

Error Handling and Debugging

Error handling and debugging are crucial aspects of writing reliable and maintainable software. No matter how experienced you are as a programmer, errors and bugs are an inevitable part of the development process. Understanding how to manage errors effectively and how to debug issues in your code will make you a more efficient and capable programmer. In this section, we will explore **Understanding Errors and Exceptions, Debugging Techniques and Tools,** and **Writing Error-Free Code.**

Understanding Errors and Exceptions

Errors and exceptions are the challenges that every programmer encounters. They can occur during runtime, compile time, or even before the program starts executing. It is important to understand the nature of these issues, their causes, and how to manage them.

Types of Errors

1. Syntax Errors:

- These are errors that occur when the program's syntax is incorrect. Syntax errors are detected by the interpreter or compiler during the compilation process, so they prevent the program from running.
- Examples include missing parentheses, incorrect indentation, or typographical errors.

Example (Python):
```python
print("Hello, World!"

# SyntaxError: unexpected EOF while parsing
```

2. Runtime Errors:

- Runtime errors happen when the program is running and typically cause the program to crash. These errors are not detected until the program is executed.
- They are often caused by issues like invalid input, trying to divide by zero, or accessing an out-of-bounds index in an array.

Example (Python):
x = 5 / 0

ZeroDivisionError: division by zero

3. Logical Errors:

- Logical errors occur when the program runs without crashing but does not behave as expected. These

are the most challenging to identify since they do not produce an obvious error message.
- ○ Logical errors can result from incorrect algorithms, wrong data handling, or erroneous assumptions in the code.

Example (Python):

```python
def add_numbers(a, b):

    return a * b  # Logical error: should be a + b


print(add_numbers(2, 3))

# Output: 6 instead of 5
```

○

Exceptions

Exceptions are a special type of error that is raised when something unexpected happens during program execution. Unlike general errors, exceptions can be explicitly handled to prevent the program from crashing.

- **Handling Exceptions**: In most programming languages, exceptions can be caught using try, catch, and finally blocks.
- **Raising Exceptions**: You can also raise exceptions manually if a particular error condition arises in your code.

Syntax (Python - Exception Handling):

try:

result = 10 / 0 # Will raise a ZeroDivisionError

except ZeroDivisionError:

print("Error: Cannot divide by zero.")

finally:

print("Execution complete.")

Common Exception Types:

- **ZeroDivisionError**: Raised when a division or modulo operation is performed with zero.
- **FileNotFoundError**: Raised when an attempt to open a file fails.
- **IndexError**: Raised when trying to access an invalid index in a list or array.
- **TypeError**: Raised when an operation or function is applied to an object of an inappropriate type.

Debugging Techniques and Tools

Debugging is the process of finding and fixing bugs or defects in your program. It is a critical skill in software development, and mastering various debugging techniques and tools can make you more effective and efficient.

Basic Debugging Techniques

1. **Print Debugging**:

- One of the simplest and most common debugging techniques is to insert print statements throughout the code to output variable values and control flow. This allows you to track the program's execution and catch errors as they happen.

Example (Python):

```python
def divide(a, b):

    print(f"a: {a}, b: {b}")  # Debugging line

    return a / b



print(divide(10, 2))
```

2. **Using Breakpoints**:

○ A breakpoint is a tool used by debuggers to pause program execution at a specific point. This allows you to inspect the program's state, including variable values, call stacks, and memory.

○ Most integrated development environments (IDEs) allow you to set breakpoints within the code.

3. **Stepping Through Code**:

○ Stepping allows you to execute your code line by line or instruction by instruction, making it easier to locate where the code diverges from expected behavior. This technique can help pinpoint the exact location of logical errors.

4. **Code Tracing**:

○ Tracing involves carefully following the flow of execution through your program, either by reading the code manually or using logging tools. It helps to identify discrepancies in the logic.

Using Debuggers

A debugger is a specialized tool that helps identify, diagnose, and fix bugs. It typically allows you to set breakpoints, step through code, inspect variables, and evaluate expressions at runtime. Debuggers are available as standalone tools or built into IDEs like Visual Studio Code, PyCharm, or Eclipse.

- **GDB (GNU Debugger)** is a popular debugger for C/C++ programs.
- **PDB (Python Debugger)** is the built-in debugger for Python, allowing you to pause code execution, inspect variables, and step through code.

Basic Debugger Commands (Python - PDB):

import pdb

```
def divide(a, b):

    pdb.set_trace()  # Set a breakpoint

    return a / b


divide(10, 0)
```

Once you run the code, the debugger will pause at set_trace(), allowing you to inspect the program's state.

Logging for Debugging

Logging is an important debugging tool that provides a more permanent record of what the program is doing. Unlike print debugging, logs can be written to files or external systems, helping track issues in production environments.

- Use **logging levels** (e.g., DEBUG, INFO, WARNING, ERROR, CRITICAL) to filter the importance of the messages.

Example (Python - Logging):

```python
import logging

# Set up logging
logging.basicConfig(level=logging.DEBUG)

def divide(a, b):
    logging.debug(f"Dividing {a} by {b}")
    if b == 0:
        logging.error("Division by zero attempt!")
        return None
    return a / b

print(divide(10, 0))
```

Writing Error-Free Code

While errors are inevitable, adopting best practices can significantly reduce the likelihood of encountering them in the first place. Writing clean, maintainable, and error-free code involves a combination of preventive measures, good design, and the use of tools.

Best Practices to Prevent Errors

1. Input Validation:

- Ensure that all inputs are validated before processing. This includes checking for data type mismatches, invalid values, and boundary conditions.

Example (Python):

```python
def safe_divide(a, b):

    if b == 0:
```

```
raise ValueError("Cannot divide by zero")

return a / b
```

2. Avoiding Hard-Coding:

- o Hard-coding values directly into the program can lead to errors if those values change in the future. Use variables or constants to make your code more flexible.

3. Consistent Naming Conventions:

- o Use meaningful variable and function names that clearly indicate their purpose. This can make your code more readable and reduce the chance of making logical errors.

4. Modular Programming:

- o Break your program into smaller, reusable modules or functions. This makes the code easier to test, debug, and maintain.

5. **Code Reviews**:

   o Regular code reviews are an excellent way to catch errors early. Having another set of eyes look over your code can help identify issues you may have missed.

6. **Automated Testing**:

   o Use unit tests to check if individual components of your program are working as expected. Writing tests ensures that your code behaves correctly and helps prevent regression bugs when changes are made.

7. **Exception Handling**:

   o Implement comprehensive exception handling to manage errors gracefully. By anticipating common errors and handling them effectively, you can ensure your program continues running smoothly.

8. **Use Linting Tools**:

   o Linting tools can automatically detect syntax and style errors in your code before execution. Tools like **Pylint** (Python), **ESLint** (JavaScript), or **SonarLint** (multilingual) can help ensure your code follows best practices.

Summary

Error handling and debugging are fundamental skills for every programmer. By understanding the types of errors that can occur, mastering techniques for debugging, and following best practices to write error-free code, you can drastically improve the quality and reliability of your software. Incorporating tools like debuggers, loggers, and automated testing into your workflow will help you identify and resolve issues efficiently, ensuring that your code is robust and user-friendly. Writing error-free code may not be fully achievable at first, but with practice and persistence, it will become a cornerstone of your programming process.

Introduction to Web Development

Web development is the process of creating websites or web applications that run on the internet. It involves a wide range of activities, from designing the visual elements and layout of a website to programming its functionality. Web development has evolved significantly, and today, it is one of the most crucial skills for developers in a world that increasingly relies on the internet.

In this section, we will dive into the basics of web development, focusing on **HTML, CSS, and JavaScript Basics**, an **Overview of Backend Development**, and how **Frontend and**

Backend work together to create dynamic and interactive websites.

HTML, CSS, and JavaScript Basics

To begin with, it's essential to understand the three primary technologies that drive web development: HTML, CSS, and JavaScript. These are the building blocks of the web, and together, they allow developers to create interactive, visually appealing, and functional websites.

1. HTML (Hypertext Markup Language)

HTML is the foundation of all web pages. It is a markup language that structures the content of a webpage. HTML consists of elements (often called tags), which define different types of content, such as headings, paragraphs, images, links, tables, and forms. The main purpose of HTML is to organize content and make it accessible to users.

Structure of an HTML Page: Every HTML page starts with a DOCTYPE declaration, followed by the opening and closing <html> tags, the <head> section, and the <body> section, which contains the content of the page.

Example:

```
<!DOCTYPE html>

<html lang="en">

<head>

    <meta charset="UTF-8">

    <meta name="viewport"
content="width=device-width,
initial-scale=1.0">

    <title>My First Web Page</title>

</head>

<body>

    <h1>Welcome to My Web Page</h1>
```

<p>This is a basic webpage using HTML.</p>

<a href="https://www.example.com">Visit Example</a>

</body>

</html>

- o **HTML Elements**: Tags such as \<h1\>, \<p\>, \<a\>, \<img\>, etc., represent elements that structure the content.
- o **Attributes**: Tags can have attributes that modify their behavior. For example, the \<a\> tag has the href attribute that specifies the link's destination.

2. CSS (Cascading Style Sheets)

CSS is a stylesheet language used to control the appearance of a webpage. It allows you to add styles, such as colors, fonts, spacing, and positioning, to HTML elements. While HTML provides the structure of the page, CSS defines how that structure should look.

CSS Syntax: CSS consists of rules that select an HTML element and apply styles to it. A rule is made up of a **selector** and a **declaration block**.

Example:

```
body {

    background-color: lightblue;

    font-family: Arial, sans-serif;

}


h1 {

    color: darkblue;

}
```

```
p {

    font-size: 16px;

    line-height: 1.5;

}
```

- o **Selectors**: These are the HTML elements (e.g., h1, p, body) you want to style.
- o **Declarations**: These define the styling properties, such as color, font size, and margin. Each declaration is written as a property: value pair.
- o **External, Internal, and Inline CSS**: You can include CSS in three different ways—externally via a separate .css file, internally within a <style> tag in the HTML document,

or inline directly within an HTML element using the style attribute.

3. JavaScript

JavaScript is a programming language used to create dynamic and interactive web pages. It runs on the client side (in the user's browser) and enables websites to respond to user actions without requiring a page refresh. JavaScript can be used for a wide range of tasks, such as form validation, animations, event handling, and interacting with APIs.

Basic Syntax: JavaScript syntax consists of variables, functions, conditionals, loops, and objects. It is an event-driven language that runs when specific events are triggered.

Example:

```
<button onclick="changeText()">Click me</button>
```

```
<script>

  function changeText() {

document.getElementById("demo").innerHTML
= "Hello, JavaScript!";

  }

</script>

<p id="demo">This text will change.</p>
```

- ○ **Variables and Functions**:
  JavaScript variables store values,
  and functions are blocks of code
  that perform tasks. Functions are
  typically executed when triggered
  by an event (e.g., button click).
- ○ **Event Handling**: JavaScript can
  listen for events, such as clicks or
  key presses, and execute a function
  when the event occurs.

- ○ **DOM Manipulation**: JavaScript interacts with the **Document Object Model (DOM)**, which represents the structure of an HTML document. You can use JavaScript to dynamically update the content of a page.

Backend Development Overview

While frontend development is responsible for creating the visual aspects of a website, **backend development** focuses on the server-side operations—managing data, handling user requests, and ensuring that everything works behind the scenes. Backend development typically involves databases, server-side scripting, and server management.

1. What is Backend Development?

Backend development is concerned with building and maintaining the server, database, and application that drive a website. It handles the logic, database interactions, and server configurations necessary to power a website's functionality.

- **Server-Side Languages**: Backend development uses languages like **Node.js**, **Python**, **PHP**, **Ruby**, **Java**, and **C#**. These languages handle tasks such as routing, data processing, and communicating with the database.
- **Databases**: Backend systems often rely on databases to store and manage data. There are two main types of databases:
  - **Relational Databases** (e.g., MySQL, PostgreSQL) store data in tables with predefined relationships between them.
  - **NoSQL Databases** (e.g., MongoDB, Firebase) store data in formats like JSON, and are more flexible when handling large amounts of unstructured data.

2. Key Backend Concepts:

- **Routing**: Routing is the mechanism that determines how a web server responds to requests for different URLs or endpoints. Backend frameworks (e.g., **Express.js**, **Django**, **Ruby on Rails**) handle routing for web applications.
- **APIs (Application Programming Interfaces)**: APIs allow different software systems to communicate with each other. Web APIs are often used to connect the frontend with the backend, enabling dynamic content loading and data interaction between the server and the client.
- **Authentication and Authorization**: Backend systems often handle user authentication (verifying user identity) and authorization (granting access to specific resources).

Connecting Frontend and Backend

In modern web development, the frontend and backend need to work together seamlessly to create a dynamic and interactive experience for users. Connecting these two parts of a web application is typically achieved through APIs and communication protocols.

1. Frontend and Backend Communication:

The frontend (client-side) and backend (server-side) communicate primarily through **HTTP requests**. When a user interacts with a webpage, the frontend sends a request to the backend to retrieve or manipulate data. The backend then responds with the requested data, and the frontend displays it.

- **HTTP Requests**: Frontend makes **GET** requests to fetch data, **POST** requests to send data, **PUT** or **PATCH** requests to update data, and **DELETE** requests to remove data.

AJAX (Asynchronous JavaScript and XML): AJAX is a technique that allows the frontend to send and receive data from the server asynchronously without reloading the page. AJAX uses JavaScript's **XMLHttpRequest** or the modern **Fetch API** to interact with the backend.

Example (Using Fetch API in JavaScript):

```
fetch('https://api.example.com/data')

  .then(response => response.json())

  .then(data => console.log(data))

  .catch(error => console.error('Error:', error));
```

2. RESTful APIs:

- **REST (Representational State Transfer)** is an architectural style for creating APIs. RESTful APIs use standard HTTP methods (GET, POST, PUT,

DELETE) to perform CRUD (Create, Read, Update, Delete) operations on data.

JSON (JavaScript Object Notation) is typically used as the data format for communication between frontend and backend.

Example (REST API Call):

```
fetch('https://api.example.com/user/123', {

    method: 'GET',

    headers: {

        'Content-Type': 'application/json'

    }

})

.then(response => response.json())

.then(data => console.log(data));
```

3. WebSockets and Real-Time Communication:

WebSockets provide a full-duplex communication channel between the client and server. They allow for real-time communication, making it possible to send and receive data instantly without refreshing the page.

- **Use Cases**: WebSockets are used in chat applications, online gaming, real-time notifications, and other applications that require live data exchange.

Summary

Web development is an exciting and ever-evolving field. To build a modern, interactive website or application, you need to understand the roles of frontend and backend development. By mastering HTML, CSS, and JavaScript, you can create the visual and interactive aspects of a website. Learning about backend development, including server-side programming and databases, allows you to create the systems that power websites. Finally, knowing how to connect the frontend and backend through APIs, HTTP requests, and real-time technologies helps you create dynamic and fully functional web applications.

Working with Databases

Databases are essential for modern web and software applications. They are systems used to store, retrieve, and manage data efficiently. Whether you're developing a web application, an enterprise-level solution, or even a simple mobile app, understanding how to work with databases is crucial for any developer.

In this section, we will explore the different types of databases, including **SQL and NoSQL** databases, the fundamental **CRUD operations**, and how to **connect code to databases** to manage data effectively.

Introduction to SQL and NoSQL

Databases are generally classified into two broad categories: **SQL** (Structured Query Language) databases and **NoSQL** (Not Only SQL) databases. Both have their strengths and are suitable for different use cases.

1. SQL (Structured Query Language) Databases

SQL databases are relational databases that use a structured query language (SQL) to interact with the data. These databases organize data into **tables** with rows and columns. SQL databases are known for their ability to handle structured data with predefined schemas and enforce data integrity through constraints like primary keys, foreign keys, and unique constraints.

- **Key Features of SQL Databases**:
  - **Relational Data Model**: SQL databases use tables, rows, and columns to organize data.

- ○ **Schema-Based**: A schema defines the structure of the data (e.g., what data types each column will store).
- ○ **ACID Properties**: SQL databases ensure data consistency and reliability with **Atomicity, Consistency, Isolation**, and **Durability**.
- ○ **Examples**: MySQL, PostgreSQL, Microsoft SQL Server, Oracle Database.

2. NoSQL (Not Only SQL) Databases

NoSQL databases are non-relational databases that provide flexible, scalable, and fast ways to store data. They are designed for applications that require high-performance, large-scale data storage, or data that doesn't fit well into traditional relational models.

- • **Key Features of NoSQL Databases**:

  - ○ **Schema-Less**: NoSQL databases don't require a fixed schema, which

makes them highly flexible and
adaptable.

- o **Scalability**: NoSQL databases are
  designed to scale horizontally,
  making them ideal for handling
  large amounts of data or traffic.
- o **Types of NoSQL Databases**:
  - ■ **Document-Based**: Stores
    data as JSON-like
    documents. Examples:
    MongoDB, CouchDB.
  - ■ **Key-Value Stores**: Data is
    stored as key-value pairs.
    Examples: Redis, Riak.
  - ■ **Column-Family Stores**:
    Data is stored in columns
    rather than rows. Examples:
    Apache Cassandra, HBase.
  - ■ **Graph Databases**: Designed
    for data with complex
    relationships. Examples:
    Neo4j, ArangoDB.
- **When to Use NoSQL**:

- When data is semi-structured or unstructured.
- For real-time web applications, such as chat applications or social media.
- For applications that require massive scalability and flexibility.

3. Comparing SQL and NoSQL

Feature	SQL (Relational)	NoSQL (Non-Relational)
Data Model	Tables with rows and columns	Flexible models: document, key-value, graph

Schema	Fixed schema with predefined structure	Schema-less, dynamic schema
Scalability	Vertical scaling (scale up)	Horizontal scaling (scale out)
Transactions	ACID-compli ant (strong consistency)	BASE-compli ant (eventual consistency)
Examples	MySQL, PostgreSQL, Oracle, SQL Server	MongoDB, Cassandra, Neo4j, Redis

CRUD Operations Explained

CRUD is an acronym that stands for **Create**, **Read**, **Update**, and **Delete**. These operations form the foundation of interacting with databases. Every database system, whether SQL or NoSQL, supports these operations to manage data.

1. Create

The **Create** operation is used to insert new records (rows in SQL, documents in NoSQL) into the database.

SQL: The INSERT statement is used to add new data to a table.

```
INSERT INTO users (name, email, age)
VALUES ('John Doe', 'john.doe@example.com', 30);
```

NoSQL (MongoDB Example): In MongoDB, you can insert a new document using the insertOne() method.

```
db.users.insertOne({ name: "John Doe", email: "john.doe@example.com", age: 30 });
```

2. Read

The **Read** operation retrieves data from the database based on specific queries. It is used to fetch and display data from the database.

SQL: The SELECT statement is used to query the database.

```
SELECT * FROM users WHERE age > 25;
```

NoSQL (MongoDB Example): In MongoDB, you use the find() method to retrieve documents.

```
db.users.find({ age: { $gt: 25 } });
```

3. Update

The **Update** operation modifies existing records in the database.

SQL: The UPDATE statement is used to modify data in a table.

```
UPDATE users

SET age = 31

WHERE name = 'John Doe';
```

NoSQL (MongoDB Example): In MongoDB, the updateOne() or updateMany() method is used to update documents.

```
db.users.updateOne({ name: "John Doe" }, {
$set: { age: 31 } });
```

4. Delete

The **Delete** operation removes records from the database.

SQL: The DELETE statement is used to remove data from a table.

```
DELETE FROM users WHERE name = 'John Doe';
```

NoSQL (MongoDB Example): In MongoDB, the deleteOne() or deleteMany() method is used to delete documents.

```
db.users.deleteOne({ name: "John Doe" });
```

Connecting Code to Databases

To work with databases from your application code, you need to connect the database to your programming language. This is typically done through **database drivers** or **ORMs (Object-Relational Mappers)** that abstract the database interaction and allow you to perform CRUD operations.

1. Connecting to SQL Databases

To connect to SQL databases like MySQL, PostgreSQL, or SQL Server, you can use a variety of programming languages and their respective libraries or modules.

Python (using mysql-connector for MySQL):

```
import mysql.connector


conn = mysql.connector.connect(

    host="localhost",

    user="root",

    password="password",
```

```python
    database="test_db"
)


cursor = conn.cursor()

cursor.execute("SELECT * FROM users")

result = cursor.fetchall()


for row in result:

    print(row)


conn.close()
```

Node.js (using pg for PostgreSQL):

```javascript
const { Client } = require('pg');
```

```
const client = new Client({

    user: 'user',

    host: 'localhost',

    database: 'test_db',

    password: 'password',

    port: 5432,

});


client.connect();


client.query('SELECT * FROM users', (err, res)
=> {

    console.log(res.rows);

    client.end();

});
```

2. Connecting to NoSQL Databases

For NoSQL databases like MongoDB, the process is slightly different, and you typically use drivers or libraries provided by the database provider.

Node.js (using mongoose for MongoDB):

```
const mongoose = require('mongoose');
```

```
mongoose.connect('mongodb://localhost:27017/test_db', { useNewUrlParser: true, useUnifiedTopology: true });
```

```
const userSchema = new mongoose.Schema({
    name: String,
    email: String,
    age: Number
```

```
});


const User = mongoose.model('User',
userSchema);


User.find({}, (err, users) => {

    if (err) throw err;

    console.log(users);

});
```

Python (using pymongo for MongoDB):

```
from pymongo import MongoClient


client =
MongoClient('mongodb://localhost:27017/')
```

```
db = client.test_db

collection = db.users


users = collection.find()

for user in users:

    print(user)
```

3. Using ORM for SQL Databases

ORMs allow you to interact with your SQL database using the programming language's native objects and classes, abstracting away the raw SQL code. Some popular ORMs include:

- **Python**: SQLAlchemy, Django ORM
- **Node.js**: Sequelize, TypeORM
- **Ruby**: ActiveRecord

Using an ORM, you can perform database operations by manipulating objects directly rather than writing raw SQL queries.

Example with SQLAlchemy in Python:

```
from sqlalchemy import create_engine, Column,
Integer, String

from sqlalchemy.ext.declarative import
declarative_base

from sqlalchemy.orm import sessionmaker


Base = declarative_base()


class User(Base):
    __tablename__ = 'users'
    id = Column(Integer, primary_key=True)
    name = Column(String)
    email = Column(String)
    age = Column(Integer)
```

```python
engine = create_engine('sqlite:///test.db')

Base.metadata.create_all(engine)


Session = sessionmaker(bind=engine)

session = Session()


# Create a new user

new_user = User(name="John Doe",
email="john.doe@example.com", age=30)

session.add(new_user)

session.commit()


# Query the users table

users = session.query(User).all()

for user in users:
```

```
print(user.name, user.email)


session.close()
```

Summary

Working with databases is a critical skill for any developer. Whether you're using a relational **SQL database** for structured data or a **NoSQL database** for flexible, large-scale applications, understanding how to perform **CRUD operations** and **connect your code to databases** is essential for building data-driven applications. By mastering database connections and queries, you can effectively store, retrieve, and manipulate data in your software projects.

APIs and Integrations

In the modern world of software development, **APIs (Application Programming Interfaces)** have become an essential tool for building powerful applications and integrating services across platforms. APIs allow different software systems to communicate with each other and share data in a standardized way, enabling developers to leverage existing services, streamline workflows, and enhance the functionality of their applications.

This section will provide an extensive overview of what APIs are, how to consume and interact with them (focusing on **RESTful APIs**), and how to build your own API to facilitate integration with other applications.

What Are APIs?

At a high level, an **API** is a set of defined rules and protocols that allow one piece of software to interact with another. APIs can be thought of as a "bridge" that enables communication between different applications, services, or platforms. They allow for the exchange of data, commands, or services in a way that is understandable and usable by both parties.

How Do APIs Work?

APIs work by exposing a set of functions, endpoints, and methods that other applications can call or use. When you make a request to an API, you're asking the service to perform a certain action, such as retrieving data, processing an action, or returning a response. The service then sends a response in the form of data, usually in a structured format such as **JSON** (JavaScript Object Notation) or **XML** (eXtensible Markup Language).

- **Request**: An application sends a request to the API endpoint, typically through an HTTP request (GET, POST, PUT, DELETE).
- **Processing**: The API server processes the request and performs the desired action.
- **Response**: The API sends a response back to the calling application, usually containing the requested data or a success/error message.

Why Are APIs Important?

APIs are important for several reasons:

1. **Data Sharing**: APIs allow different applications to share data. For example, you might use a weather API to fetch current weather information and display it on your website.
2. **Service Integration**: APIs enable seamless integration between different services. For example, integrating payment gateways (like PayPal or Stripe) into your website.

3. **Platform Independence**: APIs allow communication between different systems, regardless of the underlying platform. For example, you can integrate an Android app with a web service built on a different platform.
4. **Efficiency and Speed**: APIs allow developers to use existing services and data, speeding up the development process and making applications more efficient.

Consuming RESTful APIs

One of the most popular types of APIs in modern web development is **RESTful APIs** (Representational State Transfer). These APIs use the standard HTTP protocol and rely on stateless communication between the client and server. RESTful APIs follow a set of architectural principles and are widely used because of their simplicity and scalability.

1. Understanding RESTful APIs

RESTful APIs use simple HTTP methods to interact with resources, which are identified by **URLs (Uniform Resource Locators)**. These methods are:

- **GET**: Retrieves data from the server.
- **POST**: Sends data to the server to create a new resource.
- **PUT**: Updates an existing resource on the server.
- **DELETE**: Removes a resource from the server.

Resources in RESTful APIs are often represented in **JSON** or **XML** format.

2. Making a Request to a RESTful API

To interact with a RESTful API, you'll need to make an HTTP request to an API endpoint. Endpoints are specific URLs that represent the resources or data that you want to interact with. For example:

GET Request (Retrieve Data): Requesting a list of users.

GET https://api.example.com/users

POST Request (Create Data): Adding a new user.

POST https://api.example.com/users

Body: {"name": "John Doe", "email": "john.doe@example.com"}

PUT Request (Update Data): Updating an existing user.

PUT https://api.example.com/users/123

Body: {"name": "Jane Doe", "email": "jane.doe@example.com"}

DELETE Request (Delete Data): Removing a user.

DELETE https://api.example.com/users/123

3. Consuming RESTful APIs with Code

When interacting with APIs, you will typically send requests and handle responses using **HTTP clients** in your programming language of choice. Below is an example of how to make API calls using **JavaScript (Node.js)** and **Python**.

Example: Fetching Data with JavaScript (Node.js)

Node.js provides the axios library, which is commonly used to make HTTP requests to an API.

```
const axios = require('axios');
```

```
axios.get('https://api.example.com/users')
```

```
  .then(response => {
```

```
    console.log('User Data:', response.data);

})

.catch(error => {

    console.error('Error fetching data:', error);

});
```

Example: Fetching Data with Python (using requests)

Python's requests library is widely used for making API requests.

```
import requests


response =
requests.get('https://api.example.com/users')

if response.status_code == 200:

    print('User Data:', response.json())
```

else:

```
    print('Error fetching data:',
response.status_code)
```

4. Handling API Responses

API responses are typically in **JSON** format, though other formats (like XML) can also be used. The response usually contains:

- **Data**: The actual content you requested, such as a list of users, posts, etc.
- **Status Codes**: Indicating the success or failure of your request. Common HTTP status codes include:
    - 200 OK: Request was successful.
    - 404 Not Found: The requested resource could not be found.
    - 500 Internal Server Error: Something went wrong on the server side.

For example, a typical JSON response might look like this:

```
{

  "status": "success",

  "data": [

    {"id": 1, "name": "John Doe", "email":
"john.doe@example.com"},

    {"id": 2, "name": "Jane Doe", "email":
"jane.doe@example.com"}

  ]

}
```

Building Your Own API

Now that you understand how to consume APIs, let's discuss how you can create and expose your

own API. This allows you to provide your data
and services to other developers or applications.

1. Designing Your API

The first step in building an API is designing its
endpoints. Each endpoint corresponds to a
specific action or resource in your application.
When designing, consider:

- **Resources**: What data or entities will your
  API expose? For example, users, posts,
  comments.
- **Endpoints**: Define the endpoints for
  accessing resources. For example, /users,
  /posts/{id}, etc.
- **Methods**: Choose which HTTP methods
  will correspond to each endpoint. For
  example, a GET request on /users could
  retrieve all users, while a POST on /users
  could create a new user.

2. Building the API (Node.js Example with Express)

Here is a basic example of building a RESTful API using **Node.js** and the **Express** framework:

Install Dependencies:

```
 npm init -y
```

```
npm install express
```

1.
2. **Create API Endpoint**:

```
const express = require('express');
```

```
const app = express();
```

```
const PORT = 3000;
```

```
// Sample data
```

```
let users = [
```

```
    { id: 1, name: 'John Doe', email:
'john.doe@example.com' },
```

```
  { id: 2, name: 'Jane Doe', email:
'jane.doe@example.com' }

];


// Middleware to parse JSON data

app.use(express.json());


// GET /users: Retrieve all users

app.get('/users', (req, res) => {

    res.json({ status: 'success', data: users });

});


// POST /users: Add a new user

app.post('/users', (req, res) => {

    const { name, email } = req.body;
```

```
    const newUser = { id: users.length + 1, name,
email };

    users.push(newUser);

    res.status(201).json({ status: 'success', data:
newUser });

});


// PUT /users/:id: Update a user

app.put('/users/:id', (req, res) => {

    const { id } = req.params;

    const { name, email } = req.body;

    let user = users.find(user => user.id == id);

    if (user) {

        user.name = name;

        user.email = email;

        res.json({ status: 'success', data: user });
```

```
    } else {

        res.status(404).json({ status: 'error',
message: 'User not found' });

    }

});



// DELETE /users/:id: Delete a user

app.delete('/users/:id', (req, res) => {

    const { id } = req.params;

    users = users.filter(user => user.id != id);

    res.json({ status: 'success', message: 'User
deleted' });

});



// Start server

app.listen(PORT, () => {
```

```
    console.log(`Server running on
http://localhost:${PORT}`);

});
```

In this example, we created a simple API with the following endpoints:

- GET /users: Retrieve a list of all users.
- POST /users: Add a new user.
- PUT /users/{id}: Update an existing user's details.
- DELETE /users/{id}: Delete a user by ID.

3. Testing Your API

Once your API is up and running, you can test it using tools like **Postman** or **cURL** to make sure your endpoints are functioning correctly.

Summary

APIs and integrations are key components in building modern applications. Whether you are consuming external APIs to extend the functionality of your application or building your own API to share data and services, understanding how to work with APIs is crucial for any developer. By mastering how to design, build, and interact with APIs, you'll be able to create powerful, scalable, and connected applications that integrate seamlessly with other services and platforms.

Version Control and Collaboration

Version control is an essential aspect of modern software development. It enables developers to keep track of changes made to the code, collaborate with others, and maintain a history of revisions. Whether working on small personal projects or large teams, version control systems (VCS) allow you to efficiently manage your codebase, revert changes, and collaborate with others.

Introduction to Git and GitHub

Git is a distributed version control system (VCS) that enables developers to track and manage changes to their codebase. Git was created by **Linus Torvalds** in 2005 to support the development of the Linux kernel. Since then, Git has become the most widely used version control system due to its speed, flexibility, and ease of use.

GitHub, on the other hand, is a cloud-based platform built on top of Git that allows developers to host repositories, collaborate with others, and manage their coding projects. GitHub provides features like pull requests, issue tracking, project boards, and more, making it an essential tool for collaboration in the modern software development world.

1. Git Basics: How Git Works

Git keeps track of changes made to files in a **repository** (or "repo"). A repository is a directory where all your code and associated files are stored, along with the history of changes. There are two types of repositories in Git:

- **Local Repository**: A copy of the project stored on your computer.
- **Remote Repository**: A version of the project stored on a server (for example, GitHub).

Git operates on a few core principles:

- **Commit**: A commit is a snapshot of the project at a particular point in time. Each commit has a unique identifier (SHA hash) and contains metadata such as the author, date, and a commit message.
- **Branch**: A branch is a separate line of development that allows developers to work on new features or bug fixes without affecting the main codebase (usually called the "main" or "master" branch).
- **Merge**: Merging is the process of combining two branches back together. This allows changes made in one branch to be integrated into another branch.

- **Clone**: Cloning a repository means creating a copy of the repository from a remote source (e.g., GitHub) to your local machine.
- **Push/Pull**: Pushing refers to uploading your changes to a remote repository, while pulling refers to downloading changes from a remote repository to your local machine.

2. GitHub: Collaborating in the Cloud

GitHub makes it easy to share your repositories with others and collaborate on projects. You can:

- **Fork a Repository**: Forking allows you to create your own copy of someone else's repository. This is useful if you want to contribute to an open-source project or work on a personal project based on another's work.
- **Pull Requests**: A pull request (PR) is a proposal to merge changes from one branch into another. Pull requests allow other developers to review, comment on,

and suggest changes to your code before it's merged.

- **Issues**: GitHub issues are used to track bugs, tasks, or feature requests. Developers can create, comment on, and assign issues to specific team members.
- **Projects**: GitHub provides project management tools such as kanban boards, where you can organize tasks and collaborate with your team on project milestones.

Version Control Best Practices

Using version control effectively requires more than just knowing how to commit code. It's important to follow best practices to ensure that the development process remains organized and that the codebase remains maintainable.

1. Write Descriptive Commit Messages

Commit messages are crucial for understanding the history of a project. Good commit messages help your team (and future collaborators) understand the purpose of each change made to the codebase. A well-structured commit message should include:

- A **brief summary** of the changes (usually in the present tense).
- A **detailed description** of why the changes were made, if necessary.

Example:

Add login validation to prevent empty username submission

- Added validation to the login form to check that the username field is not empty before submitting.

- Updated the error message to be more descriptive.

2. Commit Frequently, But Not Excessively

It's important to commit often, especially when you complete a logical step or feature. However, avoid committing code every time you make a small change (such as fixing a typo). Each commit should represent a meaningful change in the project.

3. Branch Often

Use branches for new features, bug fixes, and experimental changes. This ensures that the main branch always contains stable and tested code, while work on new features can be done in isolation.

- **Feature Branches**: When starting a new feature, create a branch specifically for that feature. Once the feature is complete and tested, merge it back into the main branch.
- **Bug Fix Branches**: Similarly, when fixing a bug, create a separate branch, work on the fix, and then merge it back when it's complete.

4. Avoid Large Pull Requests

Pull requests should be manageable. Large pull requests that contain hundreds or thousands of lines of code can be difficult to review and are prone to errors. Keep your pull requests focused on a single change or feature, and make them as small and incremental as possible.

5. Keep Your Branches Up-to-Date

If you're working on a feature branch, make sure to frequently pull the latest changes from the main branch to avoid conflicts. This practice helps ensure that your code is always up to date with the rest of the project and prevents merging issues later on.

git checkout main

git pull origin main

git checkout feature-branch

git merge main

6. Use .gitignore Files

A .gitignore file is used to specify which files or directories should not be tracked by Git. Common files to ignore include build artifacts, configuration files containing sensitive information, or IDE-specific files (e.g., .vscode, .idea).

Example .gitignore:

node_modules/

dist/

.env

*.log

7. Keep History Clean

While rebasing and squashing commits can be useful tools for cleaning up the commit history, use them judiciously. Avoid rewriting history on shared branches, as this can cause conflicts for other developers. When working with feature branches, squashing commits before merging can help maintain a clean and linear project history.

Collaborating on Coding Projects

Collaboration is an essential aspect of modern software development. Version control systems like Git, combined with platforms like GitHub, make it easier to work with teams, share code, and contribute to open-source projects.

1. Forking and Cloning Repositories

When collaborating on a project, you'll often need to fork a repository or clone it. Forking allows you to create your own copy of someone else's project, while cloning downloads the repository to your local machine.

Forking: Fork a repository when you want to contribute to a project without affecting the original project. After forking, you can clone your copy of the repository and begin working on it.

 git clone
https://github.com/username/project.git

- **Cloning**: Cloning is typically used when you are starting a project from an existing repository. It downloads a copy of the repository onto your local machine.

2. Branching and Pull Requests

When collaborating on a project, branching and pull requests (PRs) play a crucial role in ensuring that everyone's contributions can be reviewed and merged systematically.

Create a branch for each new feature or bug fix you work on. This keeps your changes isolated from the main branch and prevents conflicts with other developers' code.

git checkout -b feature/new-feature

Push your branch to the remote repository once you're done working on the feature.

git push origin feature/new-feature

- **Open a Pull Request**: Once your branch is pushed to GitHub, you can open a pull request to propose your changes to the main branch. Team members can then review your changes, discuss them, and suggest improvements before merging them into the main branch.

3. Resolving Merge Conflicts

Merge conflicts occur when Git is unable to automatically merge changes from two branches.

This usually happens when two developers make changes to the same part of the code.

To resolve merge conflicts:

1. **Identify the conflicting files**.

2. **Open the conflicting files** and manually merge the changes by choosing which code to keep.

Mark the conflicts as resolved by staging the changes:

git add <conflicting-file>

Commit the merge:

git commit

4. Code Reviews and Collaboration Etiquette

Effective collaboration requires communication and respect for your teammates. Here are some key points to keep in mind:

- **Submit pull requests early** for feedback, even if they are not complete.
- **Request reviews**: Assign specific team members to review your pull requests.
- **Provide clear explanations** of what your changes are and why they are needed.
- **Respect the feedback**: Incorporate feedback into your code and make necessary changes.

5. Continuous Integration (CI) and Continuous Deployment (CD)

CI/CD is an essential part of modern software development. CI ensures that every change is tested and merged automatically, while CD automates the deployment process.

By integrating **GitHub Actions** or using other tools like **Jenkins** or **Travis CI**, you can automatically run tests on your code, deploy updates, and ensure that your project remains stable.

Summary

Version control and collaboration are key components of modern software development. **Git** and **GitHub** provide powerful tools for managing codebases, collaborating with others, and maintaining the integrity of your projects. By following best practices and leveraging the power of version control, teams can work efficiently, avoid errors, and ensure their code is always in a stable and deployable state. Through effective use of version control systems and collaboration techniques, you can streamline development workflows, create high-quality software, and contribute to the success of team projects.

Introduction to Data Science and Machine Learning

Data Science and Machine Learning (ML) have emerged as two of the most transformative fields in the technology industry. With their ability to process and analyze large datasets, make predictions, and uncover patterns, these fields are revolutionizing industries ranging from healthcare and finance to entertainment and e-commerce.

Basics of Data Analysis

Data analysis is the process of inspecting, cleaning, transforming, and modeling data to discover useful information, draw conclusions, and support decision-making. Data analysis can be broken down into several key steps:

1. Data Collection

The first step in data analysis is collecting data from various sources. Data can come from:

- **Databases**: Structured data stored in systems such as relational databases (SQL-based).
- **APIs**: Online services provide APIs for retrieving data in real time (e.g., social media platforms, financial data).
- **Spreadsheets**: Simple and widely used for storing and organizing data (e.g., Excel or Google Sheets).
- **Sensors and IoT devices**: Data from devices, including weather sensors, fitness trackers, and smart devices.

The data collected must be relevant, accurate, and in a format suitable for analysis.

2. Data Cleaning

Once data is collected, it often requires cleaning. Raw data may contain errors, missing values, outliers, or duplicates. Data cleaning involves:

- **Handling missing values**: Methods include deleting records with missing values, replacing them with averages, or using imputation techniques.
- **Correcting errors**: Identifying incorrect or inconsistent data entries and correcting them.
- **Removing duplicates**: Ensuring that the data does not contain multiple copies of the same record.
- **Standardizing data**: Ensuring consistent formats for data entries (e.g., date formats, units of measurement).

3. Data Transformation

Data transformation involves converting the data into a suitable format for analysis. This might involve:

- **Normalization**: Scaling numerical values to a standard range (e.g., 0 to 1) to ensure they're comparable.
- **Encoding categorical data**: Converting non-numeric data (e.g., text labels) into numeric formats using techniques like one-hot encoding or label encoding.
- **Aggregation**: Summarizing data to get insights, like calculating averages, sums, or counts.

4. Exploratory Data Analysis (EDA)

EDA is the process of visualizing and summarizing the key characteristics of the data. This step helps to identify trends, relationships, or anomalies in the data. Common techniques include:

- **Histograms**: To visualize distributions of numerical data.

- **Scatter plots**: To identify relationships between two numerical variables.
- **Box plots**: To detect outliers and understand the distribution of data.

5. Data Visualization

Data visualization is the art of presenting data in graphical formats to make it easier to understand and analyze. Visualizations can include:

- **Line graphs**: To show trends over time.
- **Bar charts**: To compare quantities across categories.
- **Pie charts**: To represent proportions of a whole.
- **Heatmaps**: To show correlations between variables.

6. Statistical Analysis

Statistical methods help analyze and interpret data to make inferences or predictions. Techniques include:

- **Descriptive statistics**: Mean, median, mode, and standard deviation are used to describe data distributions.
- **Inferential statistics**: Hypothesis testing, confidence intervals, and regression analysis help make predictions and test assumptions about populations from samples.

Libraries for Data Science (Pandas, NumPy, Matplotlib)

The power of Data Science comes from various libraries that make data manipulation, analysis, and visualization easier. Python is one of the most widely used languages in Data Science, with libraries such as **Pandas**, **NumPy**, and **Matplotlib** forming the foundation of data analysis.

1. Pandas

Pandas is an open-source Python library used for data manipulation and analysis. It provides two primary data structures: **Series** (1D data) and **DataFrame** (2D data), which are efficient for handling and analyzing data.

Key features:

- **DataFrame Operations**: Allows for importing, cleaning, and transforming data.
- **Handling Missing Data**: Pandas has built-in methods to detect, fill, or drop missing values.
- **GroupBy**: Enables grouping data for aggregation and transformation (e.g., summing or averaging).
- **Time Series**: Provides robust functionality for working with time-series data, such as resampling and date handling.

Example of creating a DataFrame:

```
import pandas as pd

data = {'Name': ['Alice', 'Bob', 'Charlie'], 'Age': [25, 30, 35]}
```

```
df = pd.DataFrame(data)

print(df)
```

2. NumPy

NumPy (Numerical Python) is the core library for scientific computing in Python. It provides support for large, multi-dimensional arrays and matrices, as well as a variety of mathematical functions to operate on these arrays.

Key features:

- **Array Manipulation**: Efficient creation, indexing, and slicing of arrays.
- **Mathematical Functions**: Support for complex mathematical operations, including linear algebra, statistical functions, and Fourier transforms.
- **Random Sampling**: Tools for generating random data or simulating statistical distributions.

Example of creating a NumPy array:

import numpy as np

arr = np.array([1, 2, 3, 4, 5])

print(arr)

3. Matplotlib

Matplotlib is a 2D plotting library for Python that allows you to create a wide range of static, animated, and interactive visualizations.

Key features:

- **Plotting**: Support for creating line plots, bar charts, scatter plots, histograms, and more.
- **Customizability**: You can easily customize the appearance of plots, including axis labels, legends, and colors.
- **Subplots**: Matplotlib allows for creating multiple plots in a single figure (subplot).

Example of creating a simple line plot:

```
import matplotlib.pyplot as plt

x = [1, 2, 3, 4, 5]

y = [2, 3, 5, 7, 11]

plt.plot(x, y)

plt.xlabel('X-axis')

plt.ylabel('Y-axis')

plt.title('Simple Line Plot')

plt.show()
```

These libraries, along with others, make Python a powerful tool for performing data science tasks, from cleaning data to performing advanced analysis and visualizing results.

Introduction to Machine Learning Concepts

Machine Learning (ML) is a subfield of Artificial Intelligence (AI) that involves building algorithms that can learn from and make predictions based on data. ML techniques can be used for tasks like classification, regression, clustering, and more.

1. Supervised Learning

Supervised learning is the most common form of machine learning, where the algorithm is trained on labeled data. Labeled data consists of input-output pairs, where the output is the "correct answer" the algorithm is trying to predict.

Key supervised learning algorithms:

- **Linear Regression**: Used for predicting a continuous output variable (e.g., house price).
- **Logistic Regression**: Used for binary classification problems (e.g., spam detection).

- **Support Vector Machines (SVM)**: Used for classification tasks, finding the best hyperplane to separate different classes.
- **Decision Trees**: A tree-like model for classification and regression tasks.
- **K-Nearest Neighbors (KNN)**: A simple algorithm that classifies data based on its proximity to other data points.

2. Unsupervised Learning

Unsupervised learning is used when the data doesn't have labels, and the goal is to find hidden patterns or groupings in the data. In this case, the algorithm must learn the structure of the data on its own.

Key unsupervised learning algorithms:

- **K-Means Clustering**: Groups similar data points together into "clusters."
- **Principal Component Analysis (PCA)**: Reduces the dimensionality of data while preserving as much variance as possible.

- **Hierarchical Clustering**: Builds a tree of clusters to understand the data hierarchy.

3. Reinforcement Learning

Reinforcement Learning (RL) is a type of machine learning where an agent learns to make decisions by interacting with its environment. The agent receives feedback in the form of rewards or penalties based on its actions and aims to maximize the cumulative reward over time.

Key RL algorithms:

- **Q-Learning**: A model-free algorithm that learns the value of actions in various states of the environment.
- **Deep Q Networks (DQN)**: Uses deep learning to approximate Q-values in more complex environments.

4. Neural Networks and Deep Learning

Neural networks are computational models inspired by the human brain. They consist of layers of nodes (neurons) that process information and pass it through activation functions to generate output.

Deep learning, a subset of machine learning, uses deep neural networks with many layers (also known as **deep neural networks**, or DNNs) to model complex patterns in data. Deep learning excels in areas like image recognition, natural language processing (NLP), and game playing.

Coding for Automation

Automation has become an integral part of modern programming, enabling tasks that were once manual and time-consuming to be performed quickly and efficiently by machines. Coding for automation involves creating scripts that perform specific tasks automatically without human intervention. This can be done through scripting languages, powerful libraries, and frameworks designed to handle repetitive and routine operations.

Scripting Basics

Scripting is the art of writing small programs (scripts) that automate tasks by controlling other software or performing operations directly on the system. Unlike compiled languages, which must be transformed into executable programs before running, scripts are typically interpreted line by line by a scripting engine. Scripting languages are often used for automation because they allow for rapid development, flexibility, and ease of integration with existing systems.

Popular Scripting Languages for Automation

1. **Python**: One of the most popular languages for automation due to its simplicity and vast ecosystem of libraries.
2. **Bash (Shell Scripting)**: A Unix-based scripting language commonly used to automate system administration tasks and interact with the operating system.
3. **PowerShell**: A task automation framework designed for managing and automating administrative tasks in Microsoft environments.

4. **JavaScript**: While primarily used for web development, JavaScript (via Node.js) can be used to automate backend tasks and interact with servers.

Key Concepts of Scripting

Variables and Data Types: Just like in programming, scripts make use of variables to store data. These could be integers, strings, or more complex data structures.

Example in Python:

```
x = 10

name = "Alice"
```

Control Structures: Scripts use if, for, and while loops to make decisions and repeat tasks.

Example of a loop in Python:

```
for i in range(5):
```

```
print(i)
```

Functions: Functions encapsulate reusable pieces of code, making the script more modular and easier to manage.

Example of a function in Python:

```
def greet(name):

    print(f"Hello, {name}!")
```

Input and Output: Scripts often accept inputs from users or other systems and produce outputs. This could include reading from or writing to files, interacting with databases, or making HTTP requests.

Example of reading from a file in Python:

```
with open("example.txt", "r") as file:
```

```
content = file.read()

print(content)
```

Running Scripts

Once written, scripts can be executed in various environments:

- **Command Line**: Many scripts (e.g., Bash, Python) are executed from the command line or terminal.
- **Automated Scheduling**: Tools like **Cron** (on Unix-like systems) or **Task Scheduler** (on Windows) allow you to schedule scripts to run at specific times or intervals.

Automating Repetitive Tasks

Repetitive tasks, such as file management, data processing, or web scraping, are ideal candidates for automation. By writing scripts that handle these tasks, you can save time, reduce human error, and increase efficiency.

1. File Management Automation

File management is a common repetitive task that can be easily automated with scripts. For example, you may want to automate the process of moving files, renaming files, or backing up data at regular intervals.

Example: Python script to rename files in a directory:

```
import os


folder = "/path/to/directory"

for filename in os.listdir(folder):

    if filename.endswith(".txt"):

        old_name = os.path.join(folder, filename)

        new_name = os.path.join(folder, "new_" +
filename)
```

```
os.rename(old_name, new_name)
```

2. Data Processing Automation

Data processing tasks, such as cleaning, transforming, or analyzing data, are also prime candidates for automation. With libraries like **Pandas** and **NumPy** in Python, you can automate complex data manipulation tasks.

Example: Automating data cleaning using Pandas:

```
import pandas as pd
```

```
# Load data
```

```
data = pd.read_csv("sales_data.csv")
```

```
# Clean data by removing rows with missing values
```

```
cleaned_data = data.dropna()
```

```
# Save cleaned data to a new file
```

```
cleaned_data.to_csv("cleaned_sales_data.csv",
index=False)
```

3. Web Scraping

Web scraping is the process of extracting data from websites. This is useful for tasks like collecting product prices, news articles, or other information from the web. Python's **BeautifulSoup** and **Selenium** libraries make web scraping easy to automate.

Example: Automating web scraping with BeautifulSoup:

```
import requests
```

```
from bs4 import BeautifulSoup
```

```python
url = "https://example.com"

response = requests.get(url)

soup = BeautifulSoup(response.text,
"html.parser")


# Extract and print all the headings from the
page

for heading in soup.find_all(["h1", "h2", "h3"]):

    print(heading.text)
```

4. Automating Emails

Automating the process of sending emails is a
common task in business and personal
applications. Python's **smtplib** and **email**
libraries allow you to send automated emails
easily.

Example: Sending an automated email in
Python:

```python
import smtplib

from email.mime.text import MIMEText

from email.mime.multipart import
MIMEMultipart


# Setup the email parameters

sender_email = "your_email@example.com"

receiver_email = "receiver@example.com"

subject = "Automated Email"

body = "This is an automatically generated
email."


# Create the email

msg = MIMEMultipart()

msg["From"] = sender_email

msg["To"] = receiver_email
```

```
msg["Subject"] = subject

msg.attach(MIMEText(body, "plain"))


# Send the email

with smtplib.SMTP("smtp.example.com", 587)
as server:

    server.starttls()

    server.login(sender_email, "your_password")

    server.sendmail(sender_email, receiver_email,
msg.as_string())
```

5. System Monitoring and Alerts

Automating system monitoring tasks, such as checking disk space or CPU usage, and sending alerts is essential in system administration.

Example: Automating system monitoring with Python:

```
import psutil

import smtplib

from email.mime.text import MIMEText


# Check if CPU usage is above a certain
threshold

cpu_usage = psutil.cpu_percent()


if cpu_usage > 80:

    # Send an alert email

    msg = MIMEText(f"Warning: High CPU
usage detected: {cpu_usage}%")

    msg["Subject"] = "CPU Usage Alert"

    msg["From"] = "admin@example.com"

    msg["To"] = "admin@example.com"
```

```
with smtplib.SMTP("smtp.example.com",
587) as server:

    server.starttls()

    server.login("admin@example.com",
"password")

    server.sendmail("admin@example.com",
"admin@example.com", msg.as_string())
```

Working with Libraries for Automation

Several powerful libraries and frameworks have been developed to streamline automation tasks, saving you time and effort. These libraries simplify common operations like web scraping, interacting with APIs, scheduling tasks, and automating system operations.

1. Selenium (for Web Automation)

Selenium is a popular library for automating web browsers. It allows you to interact with web pages, click buttons, fill out forms, and scrape content dynamically, as if you were a user interacting with the page.

Example: Automating a login form with Selenium:

```
from selenium import webdriver

from selenium.webdriver.common.keys import Keys


# Start a browser session

driver = webdriver.Chrome()


# Open a website

driver.get("https://example.com/login")
```

```
# Locate the login elements and send keys

username_field =
driver.find_element_by_name("username")

password_field =
driver.find_element_by_name("password")


username_field.send_keys("my_username")

password_field.send_keys("my_password")

password_field.send_keys(Keys.RETURN)


# Close the browser

driver.quit()
```

2. Cron (for Scheduling Tasks)

Cron is a Unix-based tool for scheduling recurring tasks, such as running scripts at specific times. By writing simple cron jobs, you can automate tasks like backups, system updates, or data collection.

Example: Setting up a cron job to run a backup script every day at 2 AM:

0 2 * * * /path/to/backup.sh

3. Celery (for Distributed Task Automation)

Celery is a distributed task queue for Python. It is commonly used for handling asynchronous tasks in web applications, such as sending emails, processing images, or generating reports.

Example: Setting up a Celery task to send an email:

from celery import Celery

app = Celery('tasks', broker='redis://localhost:6379/0')

```
@app.task

def send_email(subject, body, to):

    # Code to send the email here

    pass
```

4. Fabric (for Remote Server Automation)

Fabric is a Python library for automating remote server administration. It allows you to run commands, transfer files, and manage multiple servers.

Example: Deploying an application to a remote server using Fabric:

```
from fabric import Connection
```

```
# Connect to the remote server
```

```
conn = Connection('remote_user@remote_host')


# Run commands remotely

conn.run('git pull origin master')

conn.run('systemctl restart my_app')
```

Advanced Topics in Programming

As programming languages and tools evolve, so too do the challenges and opportunities that come with advanced software development. Understanding these advanced topics can significantly enhance your programming expertise and allow you to tackle complex problems efficiently. In this section, we will dive into three essential advanced topics in programming: Asynchronous Programming, Memory Management and Optimization, and Multi-Threading and Parallel Programming. These concepts are crucial for creating high-performance applications and systems.

Asynchronous Programming

Asynchronous programming is a powerful paradigm that allows you to write programs that can perform tasks concurrently without waiting for each task to complete sequentially. It is especially useful for I/O-bound applications, where the program spends significant time waiting for external resources (e.g., reading from a file, making network requests, etc.).

Understanding Asynchronous Programming

In traditional, synchronous programming, operations are executed one after the other. This can lead to inefficiencies when tasks like file reading or web requests take a long time. Asynchronous programming allows tasks to be initiated and then run in the background, enabling the main program to continue executing without waiting for them to finish.

Key Concepts:

- **Concurrency**: Refers to the ability to run multiple tasks at the same time. While these tasks may not necessarily run simultaneously, they can be interleaved efficiently to create the appearance of parallel execution.

- **Non-blocking**: In asynchronous programming, a non-blocking function is one that allows the program to continue running while it is waiting for a task to complete. This prevents the program from being "stuck" while waiting.

- **Callbacks**: Functions that are passed as arguments to other functions and are executed once the main function has finished its task. Callbacks are commonly used in asynchronous programming to continue processing after a task completes.

Asynchronous Programming in Practice

In **Python,** the asyncio library is commonly used for asynchronous programming. Python's async and await keywords allow you to write asynchronous code that looks and behaves like synchronous code, making it easier to understand.

Example of asynchronous programming using Python's asyncio:

```
import asyncio


async def fetch_data():

    print("Start fetching data...")

    await asyncio.sleep(2)  # Simulate an
I/O-bound task like fetching data from a network

    print("Data fetched!")


async def main():

    task1 = asyncio.create_task(fetch_data())  #
Schedule fetch_data to run asynchronously

    task2 = asyncio.create_task(fetch_data())  #
Schedule another fetch_data task
```

```
await task1  # Wait for task1 to complete

await task2  # Wait for task2 to complete
```

```
# Run the main function to start the
asynchronous tasks

asyncio.run(main())
```

In this example, both fetch_data() functions are run concurrently, and the program does not block while waiting for data to be fetched.

When to Use Asynchronous Programming

- **Web Servers**: Asynchronous programming is perfect for web servers, where the server needs to handle many requests simultaneously. Frameworks like **Node.js** are built on asynchronous programming to efficiently handle high levels of concurrent connections.

- **I/O-bound Tasks**: When dealing with tasks that involve reading from or writing to external resources like databases or file systems, asynchronous programming can significantly speed up your application by allowing the program to perform other tasks while waiting.

Memory Management and Optimization

Memory management refers to the process of managing the computer's memory resources effectively during the execution of a program. In modern programming, efficient memory management is critical for optimizing performance and ensuring that resources are not wasted, leading to crashes or slowdowns.

Types of Memory in a Program

1. **Stack Memory**: Used for static memory allocation, such as local variables and function calls. Stack memory is managed

automatically as functions are called and return.

2. **Heap Memory**: Used for dynamic memory allocation, where objects or data structures are created during runtime. Memory in the heap must be explicitly managed and deallocated.

Memory Management Techniques

Garbage Collection: Languages like **Python, Java**, and **C#** feature automatic garbage collection, which periodically checks for objects that are no longer in use and frees their memory. However, manual memory management is still necessary in languages like **C** and **C++**.

Example in Python:

```
import gc

gc.collect()  # Explicitly trigger garbage
collection to free unused memory
```

•

Manual Memory Management: In lower-level languages like **C** and **C++**, programmers are responsible for explicitly allocating and deallocating memory. This can lead to issues such as memory leaks (forgetting to free memory) and dangling pointers (accessing freed memory).

Example in C:

```
int* ptr = malloc(sizeof(int));  // Dynamically allocate memory

*ptr = 10;                       // Use the allocated memory

free(ptr);                       // Free the memory when done
```

-

Memory Optimization Techniques

1. **Efficient Data Structures**: Choosing the right data structure for your program can save significant memory. For example,

arrays are compact and allow fast access, but **linked lists** use more memory due to the need for extra pointers.

2. **Avoiding Memory Leaks**: Properly manage memory allocations and deallocations to prevent memory from being wasted. Tools like **Valgrind** (for C/C++) can be used to detect memory leaks in your programs.

3. **Object Pooling**: Reusing objects instead of constantly allocating new memory can help reduce memory usage, especially in high-performance systems.

Performance Optimization

- **Caching**: Storing the results of expensive operations in memory (in a cache) can improve performance by avoiding redundant calculations. Libraries like **Redis** provide caching mechanisms for web applications.

- **Lazy Loading**: Only loading data when it's actually needed (lazy loading) can help reduce memory usage during the initial stages of program execution.

- **Memory Profiling**: Using tools like **memory_profiler** (Python) or **gdb** (C/C++) helps to track memory usage and detect areas that require optimization.

Multi-Threading and Parallel Programming

Multi-threading and parallel programming are key concepts for achieving high performance in applications that need to perform multiple tasks simultaneously.

Multi-Threading

Multi-threading allows a program to execute multiple threads concurrently, where each thread can perform a separate task. Multi-threading is typically used in applications that perform many I/O-bound tasks, such as web servers or user interfaces.

- **Threads**: A thread is the smallest unit of execution within a process. Multiple threads within the same process share the same memory space, allowing them to communicate easily.
- **Thread Safety**: When multiple threads access shared resources simultaneously, synchronization is required to prevent data corruption. Tools like **mutexes, locks**, and **semaphores** are used to achieve thread safety.

Example in Python using the threading module:

```python
import threading


def print_numbers():
    for i in range(5):
        print(i)
```

```
# Create two threads to run print_numbers
concurrently

thread1 =
threading.Thread(target=print_numbers)

thread2 =
threading.Thread(target=print_numbers)


# Start both threads

thread1.start()

thread2.start()


# Wait for both threads to complete

thread1.join()

thread2.join()
```

Parallel Programming

While multi-threading is useful for tasks that can be executed concurrently, **parallel programming** involves performing multiple tasks simultaneously, often on multiple processors or cores. Parallel programming is most effective in CPU-bound tasks, where the workload can be split into smaller, independent units.

- **Concurrency vs Parallelism**: While concurrency allows tasks to be interleaved on a single core, parallelism refers to executing tasks simultaneously on multiple cores or processors.
- **Parallel Libraries**: In languages like **Python**, parallelism can be achieved using libraries such as multiprocessing or **Dask**. In **Java**, **Java Concurrency API** provides tools for handling parallel tasks.

Example in Python using the multiprocessing module:

```
from multiprocessing import Pool
```

```
def square(x):

    return x * x


# Create a pool of worker processes to run the
function in parallel

with Pool(4) as pool:

    results = pool.map(square, [1, 2, 3, 4, 5])


print(results)
```

Challenges in Multi-Threading and Parallel Programming

- **Race Conditions**: When multiple threads or processes access shared data simultaneously, without proper synchronization, it can lead to unpredictable results. This is known as a race condition.

- **Deadlocks**: A situation where two or more threads are blocked forever because each is waiting for the other to release a resource.
- **Context Switching**: The operating system needs to switch between threads, and too many threads can lead to inefficiency due to the overhead of switching.

When to Use Multi-Threading and Parallel Programming

- **Multi-Threading** is ideal for I/O-bound tasks, such as network requests or file handling, where you want to continue executing while waiting for external operations.
- **Parallel Programming** is best suited for CPU-bound tasks, such as complex calculations or simulations, where you can divide the work into smaller tasks that can be processed in parallel.

Coding Step by Step

Building and Deploying Applications

Building and deploying applications is the final step in the software development lifecycle. Once your application has been designed, developed, and thoroughly tested, it's time to bring it to life, make it available to users, and maintain it for long-term use. This process involves creating executable programs, packaging and distributing your software, and deploying applications on the web for online access. These tasks are essential for ensuring your application is accessible, functional, and well-received by users.

In this section, we will cover the key aspects of **building** and **deploying** applications, including creating executable programs, packaging your software for distribution, and deploying applications to the web.

Creating Executable Programs

The first step in deploying an application is to create an executable version of it. An executable program is one that can be run by a user without requiring any source code or development environment. This process involves compiling your code into a platform-specific executable that can be distributed and run on the intended systems.

Compiling Code into Executables

Most programming languages require the source code to be compiled into an executable format before it can be executed on a computer. The process of compilation converts human-readable code into machine code, which the operating system can understand and run.

1. **Compiled Languages**: Languages like **C**, **C++**, and **Go** are compiled languages, meaning the source code is directly translated into a machine-readable executable. The output is an .exe file (on Windows) or an application bundle (on macOS and Linux) that users can run.

C Example (using GCC Compiler):

gcc myprogram.c -o myprogram

- This command compiles the myprogram.c source file into an executable named myprogram.

2. **Interpreted Languages**: In contrast, languages like **Python**, **Ruby**, and **JavaScript** are interpreted, which means

they rely on an interpreter to execute the code at runtime rather than being compiled into an executable beforehand. However, with tools like **PyInstaller** or **cx_Freeze**, you can package Python applications into stand-alone executables.

Python Example (using PyInstaller):

pyinstaller --onefile myscript.py

- This will generate a standalone executable that can be run on a target machine without needing a Python installation.

Cross-Platform Executables

When building an application, you may need to create executables for different operating systems (Windows, macOS, Linux). Some programming environments provide cross-platform support or tools to help with this:

- **Java**: Java applications are typically compiled into bytecode (.class files) which can be run on any platform with a Java Virtual Machine (JVM).
- **Electron**: For building cross-platform desktop applications using web technologies (HTML, CSS, JavaScript), **Electron** allows you to package your app as an executable for Windows, macOS, and Linux.

Packaging and Distribution

Once the executable program has been created, the next step is packaging it along with any necessary resources and dependencies, and preparing it for distribution. Proper packaging ensures that users can easily install and run the application, regardless of their technical expertise.

Packaging Applications

Packaging involves organizing the files and dependencies into a format that can be easily distributed and installed on user systems. Common formats for packaging applications include:

1. **Windows**: .exe (executable), .msi (Microsoft Installer)

   - **Inno Setup** and **NSIS** (Nullsoft Scriptable Install System) are popular tools for creating Windows installers. These installers can include the executable file, libraries, configuration files, and other resources.

2. **macOS**: .app (application bundle), .dmg (disk image)

   - For macOS applications, tools like **Xcode** or **Electron** help package the app into an .app bundle that includes all necessary resources, or

as a .dmg file that can be mounted
and installed.

3. **Linux**: .deb (Debian package), .rpm (Red
   Hat package)

   o Linux distributions use different
   packaging systems. **Debian-based
   systems** (like Ubuntu) use .deb
   packages, while **Red Hat-based
   systems** (like Fedora) use .rpm
   packages. Packaging tools like
   dpkg or **RPM** help bundle the
   application for distribution.

Dependency Management

Applications often rely on external libraries or
packages to function. When packaging an
application, it's important to include or list these
dependencies. Dependency management tools
like **pip** (for Python), **npm** (for Node.js), or
Composer (for PHP) help manage and install
these dependencies automatically during
installation.

For example, in Python, the requirements.txt file lists all the dependencies:

requests==2.25.1

numpy==1.19.5

This allows users to install all dependencies by running:

pip install -r requirements.txt

Distributing Applications

After packaging your application, the next step is distribution. There are various methods for distributing software to users:

1. **Direct Downloads**: Providing direct download links on your website or via email.
2. **App Stores**: Platforms like **Google Play**, **Apple App Store**, or **Microsoft Store**

offer centralized ways to distribute apps.
Each store has its guidelines, approval
processes, and requirements (e.g., code
signing, app review).
3. **Package Managers**: On Linux, package
   managers like **apt** or **yum** can be used to
   distribute software. For Python, **pip**
   allows developers to share Python
   packages through the **Python Package
   Index (PyPI)**.

Deploying Applications on the Web

For web-based applications, the deployment
process involves making the application
available to users through the internet. Web
deployment can range from simple static
websites to complex web applications that need
backend servers and databases.

Frontend vs Backend Deployment

Web applications can be divided into two main
parts:

1. **Frontend**: The client-side part of the web application that users interact with. It includes HTML, CSS, JavaScript, and other assets like images or fonts.
2. **Backend**: The server-side part that handles business logic, database interactions, authentication, and other operations that occur behind the scenes.

Deploying the Frontend

The frontend of your web application (HTML, CSS, JavaScript) can be deployed to a web server, which will then serve it to users when they visit the website. To deploy the frontend:

1. **Web Hosting**: Platforms like **Netlify**, **Vercel**, or **GitHub Pages** allow easy hosting of static websites. These platforms typically offer free hosting for small projects and integrate with version control systems like **Git** for automated deployments.
2. **Content Delivery Network (CDN)**: A CDN, such as **Cloudflare** or **Amazon**

CloudFront, can be used to distribute static assets globally, improving load times and reducing server load.

Deploying the Backend

For dynamic web applications, the backend code must be deployed to a server where it can handle requests and interact with databases. Common backend frameworks include **Django** (Python), **Express** (Node.js), **Ruby on Rails**, and **Spring Boot** (Java). To deploy the backend:

1. **Cloud Providers**: Cloud platforms like **AWS**, **Google Cloud**, and **Microsoft Azure** offer managed services to host your application's backend. These platforms provide virtual machines, containers (via **Docker**), and serverless options (via **AWS Lambda**, **Google Cloud Functions**) for backend deployment.

Platform-as-a-Service (PaaS): Services like **Heroku**, **Netlify**, and **Render** offer simplified deployment for web applications. Developers can push their code to these platforms, which handle provisioning, scaling, and managing the server infrastructure.

Example of deploying a Node.js app to **Heroku**:

```
heroku create myapp

git push heroku main
```

Databases and Backend Infrastructure

For dynamic web applications that require databases, the backend server typically connects to a database (such as **PostgreSQL**, **MySQL**, or **MongoDB**) to store and retrieve data. When deploying a web application:

1. **Database Hosting**: You can use managed database services such as **Amazon RDS**, **MongoDB Atlas**, or **Firebase** to host

your databases. These services offer scalability, security, and high availability for production databases.

2. **Environment Variables**: Sensitive information like database credentials, API keys, and other secrets should be stored as environment variables and not hardcoded in your application code.

Continuous Deployment

Continuous Deployment (CD) automates the deployment process, ensuring that any code changes pushed to a repository automatically trigger the deployment pipeline, keeping your application up to date. Popular CI/CD tools include **Jenkins**, **GitLab CI**, and **GitHub Actions**.

Example of a simple CI/CD pipeline with **GitHub Actions**:

name: Deploy to Heroku

on:

```yaml
  push:

    branches:

      - main


jobs:

  deploy:

    runs-on: ubuntu-latest

    steps:

      - name: Checkout code

        uses: actions/checkout@v2

      - name: Deploy to Heroku

        uses: aksharv/heroku-deploy@v1

        with:

          heroku_api_key: ${{
secrets.HEROKU_API_KEY }}
```

```
heroku_app_name: "myapp"
```

This will automatically deploy the application to **Heroku** every time there is a push to the main branch.

Best Practices for Programmers

Programming is more than just writing code that works—it's about writing code that is clean, maintainable, and efficient. As you advance in your career as a developer, it becomes crucial to follow best practices that make your codebase easier to work with, improve collaboration, and ensure long-term sustainability.

In this section, we'll explore best practices in **writing clean and maintainable code, code documentation and comments,** and **time management and productivity tips** for programmers. These practices will help ensure that your projects are organized, readable, and easily maintainable by you and your colleagues.

Writing Clean and Maintainable Code

Clean code is code that is easy to read, understand, and modify. It avoids unnecessary complexity and follows consistent conventions. Writing clean code is vital for maintaining and scaling projects, as it ensures that future developers can quickly understand the codebase and make changes when necessary.

1. Consistent Naming Conventions

One of the cornerstones of clean code is choosing clear, descriptive names for variables, functions, classes, and other elements. When naming things in your code, always use names that make it immediately clear what they represent or what they do.

- **Variables**: Choose descriptive names for variables that represent their purpose. For example, totalAmount is clearer than a, and customerName is better than name.

- **Functions and Methods**: Use action verbs for functions that perform operations, such as calculateTotal(), fetchData(), or validateInput().

- **Classes**: Name classes in a way that describes what they represent, like UserAccount or ProductService.

2. Follow Consistent Code Formatting

Adopting a consistent coding style is essential for readability and maintainability. Consistent formatting allows others (and even yourself) to follow the logic of your code without distractions.

- **Indentation**: Always use consistent indentation to show the structure of the code. Most developers use 2 or 4 spaces for indentation, but you should settle on one style and use it consistently across the entire project.

- **Line Length**: Avoid long lines of code that extend beyond the screen width. Break up long lines into smaller, more readable parts.

- **White Space**: Use blank lines to separate logical sections of code. Group related methods and functions together and leave a blank line between unrelated sections.

3. Avoid Duplicate Code

Repetition in code leads to maintenance nightmares. If you find yourself repeating the same logic or code in multiple places, consider creating a function or class to handle it. This practice, called **DRY** (Don't Repeat Yourself), helps prevent bugs and makes the code easier to update.

For example, instead of writing out the same piece of code to validate an email address in multiple places, write a single function that performs the validation and call that function whenever needed.

4. Keep Functions and Methods Small

Each function or method should perform a single task or solve one specific problem. If a function is too long or complex, break it into smaller, more manageable pieces. This increases the readability of your code and makes it easier to debug.

- **Example**: Instead of having a function called processTransaction() that handles the entire process of payment validation, calculation, logging, and response, you could break it into separate functions like validatePayment(), calculateTotal(), and logTransaction().

5. Minimize Dependencies

Your code should avoid being tightly coupled to other parts of your codebase. Instead, aim for **loose coupling**, where different components or modules of your code are independent and can function on their own. This makes it easier to update or replace parts of your system without affecting others.

Code Documentation and Comments

While clean code reduces the need for excessive explanations, **code documentation** and **comments** remain important for communicating your logic, design decisions, and how certain parts of your code work.

1. Write Clear and Descriptive Comments

Comments should be used to clarify complex or non-obvious parts of your code. They should explain the "why" behind your decisions, rather than the "what," which should be obvious from your code itself.

Bad Comment Example:

```
x = x + 1  # Increment x by 1
```

Good Comment Example:

Incrementing the counter to keep track of the number of successful transactions

transaction_counter += 1

2. Documenting Functions

Each function should be accompanied by a description of what it does, its inputs, and its outputs. This can help others (or even yourself in the future) understand how to use it and what to expect from it.

Good Function Documentation Example (Python):
def calculate_tax(amount: float, tax_rate: float) -> float:

"""

Calculate the tax for a given amount based on the tax rate.

Args:

- amount (float): The total amount to apply the tax to.

- tax_rate (float): The rate of tax to apply.

Returns:

- float: The calculated tax value.

"""

return amount * tax_rate

3. Keep Documentation Updated

Outdated documentation can be just as bad as no documentation at all. Always ensure that your comments and documentation reflect the current state of the code. If you make a change to the logic of a function, update the relevant documentation to match.

4. Use Documentation Tools

For larger projects, especially those with APIs or libraries, using a **documentation generator** tool like **Sphinx** (Python) or **Javadoc** (Java) can help automate the creation of user-friendly documentation. These tools generate clean, readable documentation from your inline comments.

Time Management and Productivity Tips

Time management is a crucial aspect of being a productive programmer. Effective time management allows you to meet deadlines, avoid burnout, and maintain a high level of code quality.

1. Break Down Tasks into Smaller Chunks

Large programming tasks can be overwhelming. Instead of trying to tackle an entire feature in one go, break it down into smaller, manageable tasks. This helps you stay focused and track progress more easily.

- **Example**: If you're building a login system, break it down into tasks like:
  1. Design the UI
  2. Implement front-end validation
  3. Set up the back-end authentication system
  4. Test the authentication process

2. Use Time Blocking

Time blocking involves setting specific periods during the day for focused work. By scheduling uninterrupted time to work on a single task, you can reduce distractions and improve concentration.

For example:

- **9:00 AM - 11:00 AM**: Work on implementing login authentication

- **11:00 AM - 12:00 PM**: Review pull
  requests from team members

3. Prioritize Tasks (The Eisenhower Matrix)

Use a priority system to help you identify which
tasks need immediate attention and which ones
can wait. The **Eisenhower Matrix** divides tasks
into four categories:

1. **Urgent and important**: Do these tasks
   immediately.
2. **Important but not urgent**: Schedule
   these tasks for later.
3. **Urgent but not important**: Delegate
   these tasks if possible.
4. **Not urgent or important**: Eliminate or
   defer these tasks.

4. Avoid Multitasking

Research has shown that multitasking can
actually reduce productivity, especially when
working on complex tasks like coding. Focus on
one task at a time to ensure that you give it your
full attention.

5. Set Realistic Deadlines

While it's tempting to set aggressive deadlines to meet ambitious goals, unrealistic deadlines can lead to stress, bugs, and unfinished work. Be honest with yourself about how long tasks will take and set achievable milestones.

6. Take Breaks and Avoid Burnout

Programming requires sustained concentration, and working for long hours without breaks can lead to burnout and mistakes. Follow the **Pomodoro Technique**: Work for 25 minutes, followed by a 5-minute break, and take longer breaks (15–30 minutes) every 2–4 hours.

7. Use Tools to Boost Productivity

There are numerous productivity tools available to help you manage your time and tasks efficiently. Some of the popular ones include:

- **Trello** or **Jira**: For task management and project tracking.

- **GitHub Projects**: For managing issues and organizing your workflow.
- **Slack** or **Microsoft Teams**: For communication and collaboration with your team.

Real-World Coding Projects

Real-world coding projects are an essential way for aspiring programmers to gain hands-on experience and demonstrate their abilities to potential employers or clients. These projects not only solidify your coding skills but also teach you how to solve practical problems, manage deadlines, and work through challenges. Whether you're just starting or are looking to expand your portfolio, undertaking real-world projects can be one of the most rewarding aspects of your programming journey.

Sample Projects with Step-by-Step Guides

Starting with a simple project can be an excellent way to familiarize yourself with coding concepts and programming languages. As you gain experience, you can move on to more complex projects that require a deeper understanding of various technologies and frameworks. Below are some sample projects that can help you build a strong foundation.

1. Personal Portfolio Website

A personal portfolio website is one of the best beginner projects to help you get started with front-end development and demonstrate your skills to potential employers.

Key Skills Learned: HTML, CSS, JavaScript, Responsive Design, Web Design Principles

Step-by-Step Guide:

1. **Set up your project directory**:

    o Create a folder for your portfolio.

- ○ Inside the folder, create files for HTML (index.html), CSS (style.css), and JavaScript (app.js).

2. **Design your website layout**:

- ○ Think about the sections you want to include: Home, About, Projects, Contact, etc.
- ○ Use wireframes or design tools like Figma or Adobe XD to map out the layout.

3. **Create the HTML structure**:

- ○ Use semantic tags like <header>, <nav>, <section>, <footer>, etc.
- ○ Fill in content such as your bio, project descriptions, and contact information.

4. **Style with CSS**:

- ○ Add styling to make your website visually appealing.

- Use **Flexbox** or **Grid** for responsive layouts to ensure the site works well on mobile devices.

5. **Add interactivity with JavaScript**:

- Implement features like a responsive navigation menu or a contact form that uses JavaScript for validation.

6. **Deploy your website**:

- Use free platforms like **GitHub Pages** or **Netlify** to host your portfolio.

Challenges to Overcome:

- Learning CSS grid and Flexbox for responsive design.
- Managing browser compatibility issues.
- Troubleshooting JavaScript functionality (e.g., form validation, image sliders).

2. To-Do List Application

Building a to-do list app is a great way to get comfortable with JavaScript, DOM manipulation, and basic local storage concepts.

Key Skills Learned: HTML, CSS, JavaScript, DOM Manipulation, Local Storage

Step-by-Step Guide:

1. **Create HTML structure**:

     o Define the basic structure: input field for new tasks, a button to add tasks, and an area to display the list of tasks.

2. **Style the app with CSS**:

     o Create a clean, minimalistic design that is user-friendly.
     o Make sure the layout adapts well to various screen sizes.

3. **Implement the core functionality with JavaScript**:

     o Add functionality to add new tasks.

o Implement a system to mark tasks as completed or delete them.

4. **Use Local Storage**:

o Store the tasks in the browser's **localStorage** so they persist even when the page is reloaded.
o Load the tasks from local storage when the page is first loaded.

5. **Enhance with additional features**:

o Add options to edit tasks.
o Implement a search filter to display tasks based on keywords.

Challenges to Overcome:

• Managing dynamic DOM elements (tasks) effectively.
• Storing and retrieving data using local storage.
• Handling edge cases (e.g., empty tasks, duplicate tasks).

3. Weather App

Building a weather application involves fetching data from an external API, displaying dynamic content, and handling errors effectively. It's a great way to learn about API integration, asynchronous programming, and user interface design.

Key Skills Learned: HTML, CSS, JavaScript, Fetch API, Asynchronous Programming (Promises, async/await)

Step-by-Step Guide:

1. **Set up HTML structure**:

    ○ Include fields to enter the city name, display current weather, temperature, and other weather-related data.

2. **Style with CSS**:

    ○ Create a layout that presents the weather information clearly and neatly.

- Make the design responsive for different screen sizes.

3. **Use JavaScript to fetch weather data**:

- Use the **Fetch API** to get weather data from a public API like **OpenWeatherMap**.
- Display the weather data in the app, including temperature, humidity, weather condition, and wind speed.

4. **Implement error handling**:

- Display appropriate messages when there's an error, such as when the user enters an invalid city or when the API fails.

5. **Add additional features**:

- Allow users to view the weather forecast for the next few days.
- Use icons to represent weather conditions (sun, rain, snow, etc.).

Challenges to Overcome:

- Handling asynchronous data fetching.
- Parsing and displaying data from APIs.
- Implementing error messages and validations for user input.

4. E-commerce Website (Basic)

Creating a simple e-commerce site involves building product pages, managing a shopping cart, and implementing basic checkout functionality.

Key Skills Learned: HTML, CSS, JavaScript, API integration, Form Handling, Local Storage

Step-by-Step Guide:

1. **Create product listings**:

   o Display a list of products with prices, descriptions, and images.
2. **Design the shopping cart**:

   o Allow users to add products to their cart and view the cart.

○ Use **localStorage** to persist the cart items even if the page is refreshed.

3. **Implement checkout functionality**:

○ Create a checkout page where users can review their order and enter their details.

4. **Add product search and filters**:

○ Allow users to search for products by name, category, or price.

5. **Deploy the website**:

○ Host it using platforms like **GitHub Pages** or **Heroku**.

Challenges to Overcome:

- Managing user data (e.g., shopping cart items).
- Handling form validation and checkout steps.
- Ensuring the site is mobile-friendly and responsive.

Tips for Tackling Project Challenges

As you work through coding projects, you'll face a variety of challenges. Here are some tips to help you overcome them:

1. Break Problems Into Smaller Pieces

When faced with a complex task, break it down into smaller, manageable chunks. For example, instead of thinking about how to implement an entire feature, focus first on one part—like how to retrieve data, or how to build a user interface component. By dividing problems into smaller tasks, you make them less overwhelming.

2. Don't Be Afraid to Ask for Help

Whether you're stuck on an error or need guidance on a particular concept, don't hesitate to ask for help. There are many communities like **Stack Overflow**, **Reddit**, and **GitHub** where developers actively collaborate and help one another.

3. Google and Stack Overflow Are Your Friends

When you encounter an issue or bug, a simple search on **Google** or **Stack Overflow** can often provide a solution. Make sure to search for your specific problem along with any error messages you're receiving to find relevant answers.

4. Embrace Trial and Error

It's important to understand that coding involves a lot of trial and error. Don't be discouraged if your initial attempt doesn't work out. Debugging and refining your code is a natural part of programming.

5. Take Breaks and Come Back with Fresh Eyes

If you find yourself stuck for too long on a problem, take a break and come back to it later. Often, a fresh perspective can help you spot errors or come up with new solutions.

Building a Portfolio of Work

A strong portfolio can make a huge difference in landing a job or gaining clients as a freelance developer. Your portfolio showcases your skills and gives employers insight into the quality of your work. Here's how to build a portfolio that stands out:

1. Include a Variety of Projects

Demonstrate your range by including projects that cover different aspects of development. Include:

- Front-end projects (websites, user interfaces).
- Back-end projects (APIs, databases).
- Full-stack projects (apps that involve both front-end and back-end work).
- Other projects that interest you (e.g., machine learning, mobile apps).

2. Write Clear Descriptions

For each project, include a brief description that explains:

- What the project is.
- What technologies you used.
- Any challenges you faced and how you solved them.
- A link to the live project (if possible) and/or its GitHub repository.

3. Showcase Code Quality

Choose projects that demonstrate your ability to write clean, maintainable code. If possible, include code snippets or even full repositories on GitHub, as this shows potential employers how well you structure your code.

4. Highlight Real-World Impact

If you have worked on any real-world projects (such as freelancing or contributing to open-source), include these in your portfolio. Showing real-world applications of your skills can be a huge plus.

5. Continuously Update Your Portfolio

As you gain more experience and work on more advanced projects, keep updating your portfolio to reflect your growth. This demonstrates that you are constantly learning and improving.

Appendices

Glossary of Programming Terms

A glossary of programming terms is invaluable for beginners and even experienced programmers, as it offers quick definitions and explanations of key concepts in the programming world. Knowing the terminology is crucial to understanding documentation, tutorials, and industry discussions. Below are some key programming terms you may encounter:

1. Algorithm

An algorithm is a set of step-by-step instructions designed to perform a specific task or solve a particular problem. It's a fundamental concept in programming, helping to define the logic behind a program's operations.

2. API (Application Programming Interface)

An API is a set of functions and protocols that allows different software applications to communicate with each other. It defines the way software components should interact, often allowing for data exchange or service usage between applications.

3. Bug

A bug refers to an error or flaw in software that causes it to function improperly or crash. Bugs are usually identified and fixed through debugging.

4. Compiler

A compiler is a program that translates code written in a high-level programming language into machine code or intermediate code that a computer can understand and execute.

5. IDE (Integrated Development Environment)

An IDE is a software application that provides comprehensive facilities to computer programmers for software development. It typically includes a code editor, compiler, debugger, and other tools to aid in writing, testing, and debugging code.

6. Loop

A loop is a control structure that allows for repeated execution of a block of code. There are different types of loops, including **for**, **while**, and **do-while** loops, which repeat tasks based on specific conditions.

7. Object-Oriented Programming (OOP)

OOP is a programming paradigm based on the concept of objects, which can contain data in the form of fields and code in the form of procedures. OOP encourages the creation of reusable, modular code.

8. Recursion

Recursion is a programming technique where a function calls itself directly or indirectly in order to solve a problem. Recursive functions typically break a problem into smaller sub-problems until a base case is met.

9. Syntax

Syntax refers to the set of rules that defines the structure of valid statements in a programming language. Incorrect syntax results in errors during compilation or interpretation.

10. Variable

A variable is a storage location in a computer program that holds a value, which can be changed during the execution of the program. Variables are typically defined with a specific data type (e.g., integer, string, boolean).

11. Version Control

Version control is a system that tracks changes to code over time, allowing multiple developers to work on the same project without interfering with each other's changes. **Git** is one of the most popular version control systems.

12. Framework

A framework is a pre-built set of tools, libraries, and best practices for building software applications. Examples include **React** for front-end development and **Django** for Python-based web development.

13. Frontend and Backend

In web development, **frontend** refers to the part of the website that users interact with (the UI), while **backend** refers to the server-side of an application where data is processed and stored.

14. Data Structure

A data structure is a way of organizing and storing data so that it can be accessed and manipulated efficiently. Common data structures include **arrays, lists, trees,** and **hash maps**.

15. Framework

A framework is a pre-defined structure or platform that simplifies development by providing reusable libraries and tools. Popular frameworks include **Angular** for JavaScript and **Spring** for Java.

Cheat Sheets for Popular Languages

Cheat sheets provide quick reference guides for frequently used syntax and commands, making them an essential tool for developers during coding sessions. Below are cheat sheets for some of the most popular programming languages:

1. Python Cheat Sheet

- **Variables and Data Types**: $x = 10$ (int), name = "John" (string)
- **Control Structures**:

- ○ if condition:
- ○ for i in range(10):
- **Functions**: def function_name():
- **Lists**: my_list = [1, 2, 3], my_list.append(4)
- **Libraries**: import pandas as pd, import numpy as np

2. JavaScript Cheat Sheet

- **Variables**: let name = "Jane", const x = 5
- **Functions**: function greet() { }
- **Loops**: for (let i = 0; i < 10; i++) { }
- **Objects**: let car = { make: "Toyota", model: "Corolla" }
- **Array Methods**: array.push(), array.pop(), array.map()

3. Java Cheat Sheet

- **Variables**: int num = 10;, String name = "John";
- **Conditionals**: if (x > 10) { }
- **Loops**: for (int i = 0; i < 10; i++) { }

- **Methods**: public static void main(String[] args) { }
- **Arrays**: int[] arr = new int[5];

4. HTML/CSS Cheat Sheet

- **HTML Tags**: <h1>, <p>, <a href="url">
- **CSS Selectors**: p { color: blue; }
- **CSS Box Model**: margin, padding, border, content
- **CSS Layout**: display: flex;, display: grid;

5. SQL Cheat Sheet

- **Basic Queries**: SELECT * FROM users;, INSERT INTO table VALUES (...);
- **Filtering**: WHERE condition
- **Joining Tables**: SELECT * FROM orders JOIN customers ON orders.customer_id = customers.id;
- **Aggregations**: SELECT COUNT(*), AVG(price) FROM products;

Useful Online Resources and Communities

The world of programming is vast and constantly evolving, so staying connected with online resources and communities can provide ongoing support, education, and opportunities for collaboration. Here's a list of some valuable resources:

1. Stack Overflow

- **Website**: stackoverflow.com
- **Description**: A popular question-and-answer community for developers. You can ask questions, share knowledge, and learn from others' experiences.

2. GitHub

- **Website**: github.com
- **Description**: A platform for version control and collaborative software development. You can contribute to open-source projects, host your code repositories, and showcase your work.

3. MDN Web Docs

- **Website**: developer.mozilla.org
- **Description**: A comprehensive resource for web technologies, including HTML, CSS, and JavaScript. MDN offers tutorials, documentation, and examples to help developers at all levels.

4. W3Schools

- **Website**: w3schools.com
- **Description**: An educational website offering tutorials and references on web development topics such as HTML, CSS, JavaScript, SQL, and more. Great for beginners.

5. FreeCodeCamp

- **Website**: freecodecamp.org
- **Description**: An interactive learning platform with free courses covering web development, data science, and more. It includes hands-on coding challenges and certifications.

6. Reddit Programming Communities

- **Website**: reddit.com/r/programming
- **Description**: A large community of programmers discussing the latest trends, programming challenges, and projects. You can ask for advice, share your work, or browse discussions.

7. Codecademy

- **Website**: codecademy.com
- **Description**: An interactive platform that teaches coding through practical exercises and projects. Offers courses in languages like Python, JavaScript, and SQL.

8. Coursera and edX

- **Websites**: coursera.org and edx.org
- **Description**: Online platforms offering free and paid courses from top universities and organizations. Topics range from introductory programming to specialized fields like data science and machine learning.

9. HackerRank

- **Website**: hackerrank.com
- **Description**: A platform offering coding challenges, competitions, and interview preparation materials. It's a great place to practice coding and improve problem-solving skills.

10. Dev.to

- **Website**: dev.to
- **Description**: A community for developers to share articles, tutorials, and ideas. It's a great platform to learn, share, and collaborate on development projects.

Coding Step by Step

Coding Step by Step

Coding Step by Step

www.ingramcontent.com/pod-product-compliance
Lightning Source LLC
Chambersburg PA
CBHW071406050326
40689CB00010B/1775